A Woman's Guide to Successful Investing

JOHN M. WILLIAMS

A Woman's Guide to Successful Investing

A Helen Van Pelt Wilson Book

1975
DOUBLEDAY & COMPANY, INC.
GARDEN CITY, NEW YORK

PRINTED IN THE UNITED STATES OF AMERICA
FIRST EDITION

Library of Congress Cataloging in Publication Data
Williams, John Minors, 1924–
A woman's guide to successful investing.
"A Helen Van Pelt Wilson book."
Includes index.
1. Investments. 2. Finance, Personal. I. Title.
HG4521.W483 332.6′78
ISBN 0-385-08920-1
Library of Congress Catalog Card Number 74–2528

For My Wife
RUTH
Who has a fine hand with investments

Contents

Illustrations

A Woman and Her Money Need Not Be Soon Parted

Mine is an investment story to give any woman pause. For years I saved some of my earnings but invested them with not even the dimmest idea of what I was doing. Of course, know-how wasn't too important between 1945 and 1965, the period of a rampaging bull market when you could scarcely lose a cent unless you were madly speculative. But in those years I didn't need to know anything or to pay much attention to the handling of my investments. I lived in Philadelphia then and my lawyer, who was a close friend, with a broker who was *his* close friend, supervised my affairs. Then both men died within a few months of each other and I moved away. Hear now the unbelievable experience of an uninformed woman in strange financial territory.

First, a *friend* advised me to buy Equity Funding. (Perhaps the complete demise of that company is not known to you.) It is a horror story. On my own, I got out somewhere before the end, for people who advise you to buy almost never tell you when to sell. This friend also recommended a broker who was his *friend*. My records show that this broker never gave me one single piece of good advice; on his recommendations, I bought a lot and I lost a lot. Of course, by this time the bear market was upon us and wise investing was pretty hard to come by. Furthermore, I had not an inkling of the true function of a broker. *Honestly, I thought brokers had special knowledge.*

So, pretty confused, I took the advice of another *friend* and put my affairs into the hands of a local investment company. Perhaps this was my worst mistake; I stayed with this inept group for only a few months. When they sold my favorite stock (oh yes, I had certain emotional favorites by this time) at 117 and it subsequently went to 160 we parted—and not with compliments on my side.

The awful part of this association was that, when they sold, no attention was paid to capital gains, although full information on my costs had been given. My income tax that year was for me horrendous and, since my estimated tax the next year was based on it, that year's tax was also horrendous. By that time, in my dumb way, I at least knew enough about capital gains to oversee the buying and selling myself so that the third year I had no income tax at all to pay because I had overpaid so much the previous year.

Now behold me, thoroughly bewildered, following the advice of another *friend* who introduced me to *her* broker. I never investigated him; it never occurred to me. He was right for my friend but her objectives and her fortune were far different from mine. I now know that two stocks he bought for me were highly speculative. The first stock slid precipitously and quickly. The brokerage firm had been "lied to," I was told, and the stock was no good. Flattered into being a "good sport," I was whisked into another stock where I would quickly "make up all my loss." But that went down too. The results of these two transactions were a $4,041.58 loss for me plus $180.28 fees paid to the broker for his transactions, and today the first stock sells for a little more than the second, though both are way down.

About this time, quite desperate, I enrolled in an investment course that John Williams was giving for the sixth year at the local high school. At last light dawned and, realizing the benighted condition of many women like me who may be knowledgeable enough in their own fields but not in investing, I urged him to write this book—to put it all down in simple black and white for our benefit.

Now, as woman to woman, I urge you to "read, learn, mark, and inwardly digest" these pages. Then, if you have the time and, from this book, the knowledge to manage your investments yourself, I am sure you can do it to advantage. You may not buy on margin or try puts and calls but you will be able to buy and sell with some understanding—or simply hold off for a time as this author advises when the market is erratic.

Or, if you have no head for figures or prefer not to handle

your money yourself, with this good background information you can arrange for the trust department of your bank to do it for you for a small percentage fee. Or you can engage a personal investment counselor and, likewise for a small percentage fee, let him take over for you.

Anyway, if you have a regular $50 to invest every month or a big inheritance to place safely, be assured that a woman and her money need not be soon parted but held onto and probably increased. In recent years mine has been, and so can yours!

New Canaan, Connecticut — *Helen Van Pelt Wilson*
January 1975 — EDITOR

Making the Most of It

In the years that I have been an investment counselor and a lecturer at seminars, the same questions have been asked repeatedly. The same confusions have apparently existed concerning the different types of stocks, bonds, and bank savings and the best ways of handling these to financial advantage. Therefore this book. I believe it includes most of the answers and does not overlook the fact that it is sometimes wise not to invest but to wait while savings accounts grow so that money can be available when what appear to be worth-while opportunities present themselves.

This discussion is directed primarily to women—to business women who earn regularly and save regularly, to widows and divorcees, to women who are retired, and to the many who must suddenly assume responsibility for inherited money and are not willing to leave all decisions to executors. Also, I notice that more and more housewives are handling the family investments, sometimes along with their husbands, often by themselves. Husbands can be so busy making money that they don't have much time—or energy—left to study ways to invest it.

And it does take time to handle money properly, not a lot but enough for careful daily perusal of the financial pages of a newspaper and perhaps weekly reading of a financial publication like Barron's or a news magazine like *U.S. News & World Report.* Of course the stock market must be followed and some thought also given to what opportunities appear in the course of daily life. The business woman is naturally aware of commercial and industrial products; the homemaker notices which consumer products sell in quantity in the supermarket and what new, often excellent items make a company's stock worth investigating.

The chapter on selecting a broker was inspired by one of my clients who said she would be "embarrassed to ask a broker all those questions." Yet her account was not small and, as I pointed out, it was *her* money that was at stake. The information on margin trading was prompted by another client who misconstrued it as gambling until she understood the conservatism of trading "short against the box."

Here then is information that will not tell you how to become a millionaire but will help you to sound comfortable investing and show you how to make the most of what you have.

Westport, Connecticut
January 1975

John M. Williams

PART ONE

Places Your Money Can Work for You

CHAPTER ONE

Stocks, Common and Preferred

WHERE TO START

Your investment in the market is likely to start with stocks. Soon after, bonds may be of interest to you.

FUNDAMENTALS

Stocks and bonds are sold by a company to raise money to operate and expand a business. This need is your opportunity. First, of course, you have to know the difference between a stock and a bond.

A *stock is your investment* in a company; it gives you a part ownership; it entitles you to a share of all profits.

A *bond is your loan* to a company; it entitles you to receive interest and repayment of the loan by the company at specified times.

Stocks and bonds are referred to as securities. Together with any cash you have for additional purchases, they are referred to as your *portfolio*.

Keep in mind that a corporation is simply a legal "person." It has the same financial needs that you and I have. You probably have monthly charge accounts, possibly an eighteen-month automobile loan, a three-year home improvement loan, and a twenty-five-year mortgage. Like you, a corporation needs money for various purposes and at different times. Instead of going to a bank, the company may prefer to go to investors and sell them stocks or bonds. Just as you encounter different rates and terms, so it is that various types of securities are offered to investors.

COMMON STOCKS AND DIVIDENDS

Let's assume that you and I decide to form the Pseudo Corporation. We need $10,000—*capital*—to get started. Each of us invests $5,000 and we issue *common stock* to ourselves for that amount. We are then set up to share equally in profits and losses. This constitutes the basic structure of a corporation.

As business progresses, we may decide that more capital is required than we can afford. Additional shares of common stock can be sold to other investors; the company will thus receive the necessary cash. When this is done, our shares will be a smaller percentage of the total number of shares that have now been sold. As a result, the profits of the company, instead of being divided fifty-fifty, must now be distributed proportionately among all the shares of stock.

An owner of common stock shares in the *profits* of a company, and a portion of the profits is usually distributed four times a year as *dividends*. The more profit the bigger the dividend you are likely to receive. Of course if there is no profit there is nothing to distribute and the dividend is *omitted*.

Just as you try to put aside some of your earnings or household money for a rainy day, a corporation usually puts aside some of its profits as *retained earnings;* it does not pay them all out in dividends. Then if the company fails to make a profit one year it can still pay dividends from retained earnings. Or it may use these to finance growth. However, as long as profits increase year after year, you should also expect the dividend to be increased from time to time.

Stockholders, as owners of a company, are entitled to decide the amount of the dividend, to select the president, and to see that the company is properly run. As the number of stockholders grows, this arrangement obviously would lead to chaos. The solution is for the stockholders to elect representatives—*directors*—to perform these duties for them. The members of the *Board of Directors* usually receive a fee for their efforts but aren't necessarily employees of the company. They can be *outside directors*.

In 1973, American Telephone & Telegraph—A.T.&T.—had a total of nineteen directors of whom only three were employees of the company. The remaining sixteen came from law firms, colleges, banks, and industry. Each was a leader in his particular field, and each had a particular expertise to contribute to the management of the company.

THE ANNUAL MEETING

The Board of Directors meets as often as necessary during the year to provide continuing direction to the company management. Once a year, however, a meeting of all the stockholders is held. At this time you are entitled to vote for the election of directors and to approve or disapprove of their actions during the past year. You have one vote for each share of stock you own.

After hearing a report on company activities for the year and with the formal voting completed, you are free to ask as many questions as you want. It is your opportunity also to tell the directors how you think the company should be run. If your views are shared by many other stockholders, you can be sure the directors will not take them lightly. In recent times the directors of major corporations have been forced to include women and representatives of the public on their boards because of demands made at the annual meetings by the stockholders.

Most stockholders live too far away to be able to attend the meeting. Therefore the company sends each one an absentee ballot—a *proxy*—and at the same time advises when and where the meeting is to be held. The proxy form covers all the issues that are to be voted on and it designates an individual to cast your vote for or against the propositions as you indicate on the form.

It is important that you complete the proxy form and return it so that management will have a mandate to continue the performance of its duties. You can't complain about results if you can't be bothered to vote.

PREFERRED STOCK

Our Pseudo Corporation may operate fairly profitably for some time, but management and the directors may decide that, if the company had more money to work with, it could become much more successful. A letter explaining this is sent to us, the shareholders, and we vote at a special meeting to let the company sell *preferred stock.* The advantages of preferred stock will be obvious when you understand its features.

This class of stock assures the owner of a *specified dividend.* The amount is stated on the stock certificate sent to each shareholder. It must be paid out of profits before common stockholders can receive a dividend. In exchange for this preferential treatment, *the dividend is never increased over the amount specified,* even if profits soar. In fact, when a company is successful, dividends on common stock are often greater than those on preferred stock.

Typical is Continental Corporation, which issued both common and preferred stocks. The preferred stock has a stated dividend of $2.50 each year. In 1972 the comparable common stock paid $2.20. Profits rose and the common stock dividend was increased in 1973 to the equivalent of $2.51. In 1974 it was increased again to $2.64 per share. Regardless of how much profit is made, the preferred stockholders receive only the stated amount of dividend.

Preferred stock offers considerably less risk than common stock. If the Pseudo Corporation should go bankrupt, all property and equipment would be sold—*liquidated*—to pay debts. Any money left over would then be used to pay back the investors. Preferred stockholders would be paid first. This stock, therefore, is in a preferred position for both dividends and liquidation.

Preferred stock offers advantages to three groups: the company, which gets needed cash; the preferred stockholders, who have been induced to invest in an only moderately successful company in return for a fixed dividend and reduced risk; the common stockholders, who retain the potential for unlimited dividends. The common goal of all three is to have a healthy growing company.

CUMULATIVE FEATURE

Just as you encounter different interest rates and terms when you want to raise money to buy a house or car, so does a company. A lot depends on how badly you need the money, how good your credit is, and how many people have money to lend at the time. In other words, whether money is tight or plentiful.

The specified dividend of preferred stock is one of its attractions for investors. By itself, however, it has limited appeal, for if there are no profits, no dividend will be paid. To get around this handicap, preferred stock may include, in addition to the specified dividend, a *cumulative feature.* This provides that, if the company omits the preferred dividend owing to lack of profits, the dividend becomes a debt owed by the company. *These omitted dividends must be paid in full*—as soon as profits permit —and *before any common stock dividend is paid.* In this way, the preferred stockholder has even greater assurance of dividends —even though they may be delayed.

CONVERTIBLE FEATURE

A second inducement of preferred stock is the *convertible feature.* This provides that your preferred stock may be converted into a definite number of shares of common stock. The exact terms of conversion are spelled out by the company at the time the stock is issued. Through years of slim profits, your preferred stock will pay dividends while the common stock may not. But if profits soar and larger dividends are paid to common stockholders, you have the privilege of converting your preferred stock into common, and so receiving the bigger dividends.

The decision to sell preferred stock with either the cumulative or convertible feature or both is made by company management. Two factors influence the decision: must the features be added to arouse investor interest and thus assure the sale of all the stock; and will investors be satisfied with a slightly lower specified dividend if these desirable features are added?

DIFFERENT CLASSES OF PREFERRED

You may have heard that a company has several classes of preferred stock. These are usually identified as Preferred A, Preferred B, etc., or First Preferred, Second Preferred. The designations identify different issues of preferred stock that are issued at different times. The Preferred A might have a dividend of $1.50 per share and be convertible into two shares of common stock; Preferred B—issued later—might have a $1.80 cumulative dividend and no conversion privilege. Northern States Power Company has several preferred stocks identified all the way from Preferred A to Preferred K and paying dividends of anywhere from $3.60 to $8.80 per share.

Just as preferred stockholders have certain priorities over common stockholders, owners of one class of preferred have certain priorities over owners of another class. These priorities are spelled out at the time the stock is issued. Even so, the preferreds are more conservative than the common stock.

CALL FEATURE

A company that needs more cash for a limited time, possibly only five to ten years, can raise it by a new issue of preferred stock. Rather than commit itself to paying the preferred dividend indefinitely, the company includes a *call feature* as an aspect of the new issue. This permits the company, at the end of a stated number of years, to buy back (call) the stock and at a specified price. In return for this privilege the company usually makes the *call price* slightly higher than the original or offering price. The company may also have to pay a slightly higher dividend than would be required without the call feature.

ABOUT TAXES

Your investments are subject to two different taxes by the federal government and in some cases by state and city taxes as well. It depends on where you live. For example, New York State and New York City both impose taxes.

The dividends and interest your investments earn are subject to *income tax* just like the money you earn at a job. If your salary is $15,000 a year and you receive another $1,000 in dividends or interest, you pay federal income tax on the entire $16,000. The same holds true if your state or city has its own income tax. Also, if you pay an estimated quarterly income tax, you must include this investment income in estimating the tax.

The other tax you will suffer is the *capital gains tax*. This tax is based on the difference between the amount you paid for a security and the amount you sold it for. You don't have to worry about this tax until you *sell* your security even if it doubles or triples in value over the years you own it. If you sell your security at a loss, the loss may be deducted on your tax return.

Under some circumstances the tax rate on this profit is quite a bit less than the rate you pay on income. Under the present law, a capital gain or loss incurred on a security owned less than six months—*short term*—is treated like ordinary income. In other words, you take your regular earnings and either add or subtract your short-term capital gain or loss, and pay the appropriate tax on the total. If the gain or loss is incurred on a security owned more than six months—*long term*—only half the amount is added or subtracted.

To a considerable extent your decisions on taxes can be guided by your accountant or tax adviser, but you yourself should not be totally unaware of how your taxes are affecting your buy and sell decisions. Keep in mind from the start that in one form or another the income and profits from your investments are going to be taxed. But don't avoid switching an investment just because you will have to pay a large tax. After all, you wouldn't turn down a higher-paying job offer because you will have to pay higher taxes. If you continue to hold onto a stock for this reason, the price may decline far more than the tax you would have had to pay, and you may lose an opportunity to invest elsewhere to much better advantage. If you have doubts about tax consequences or about current tax rules, call your local Internal Revenue Service Office. Or your accountant can give you this information, possibly based on greater familiarity with your particular circumstances. Neither the I.R.S. nor an accountant should tell you to evade the taxes but they may be able to help you reduce them.

CHAPTER TWO

Opportunities in Bonds

CORPORATE, MUNICIPAL, AND GOVERNMENT

One of my clients who could discuss stocks with ease and knowledge at first foundered on bonds. She understood the bonds she had bought when they were offered at face value but went blank when I talked about the interest on bonds bought at a discount. Debentures, she declared, gave her a headache. In due course she discovered that bonds were no more difficult to understand than stocks, and at times they were a much better investment for her.

When a company needs money, it can borrow from a bank the same as you and I. But if it requires a very large loan that will take a long time to repay, the company can sell—*float*—a bond issue. *A bond is a contract to borrow money for a stated number of years at a stated rate of interest.* Bonds are usually sold in units of $1,000.

Corporate bonds

If Pseudo Corporation floats a bond issue, it might be described as 7's of '93. This means that the company will pay you 7 per cent interest per year on the borrowed money and will pay back the total in 1993—*at maturity*.

If you buy this $1,000 bond, you will be paid $35 interest twice a year—a total of $70. This is 7 per cent of the $1,000 *face value*. You collect the interest in one of two ways: if the bond is *registered*, Pseudo Corporation will send you, the registered owner, a check every six months; if it is a *bearer*—or *coupon*—*bond*, your bond certificate will carry coupons. You cut off one of these every six months and send it to your bank for deposit in your account. The bank will collect the amount from Pseudo Corporation just as it would a check.

Registered bonds are the safer. Not only are they more convenient, but they are not negotiable in case of loss or theft. Your name is registered on the face of the bond certificate as well as on the company records.

Bearer bonds belong to any bearer or holder. In case of loss, they may be sold by anyone who finds them, since there is no record of who the rightful owner is. The coupons are also fully negotiable, and each one shows the amount of interest and the date it is due. When you buy a bearer bond, make sure *all* the coupons are there and none mistakenly removed by the previous owner.

Even though interest is paid only twice a year, your money is earning interest every day you own the bond. Suppose you sell your bond five months after receiving the interest. You are still entitled to interest for those five months. The new purchaser of the bond, therefore, pays you not only the sale price but also the five months' interest. As the new owner, you will receive the full six months' interest when you cut the next coupon or the company sends you the next payment when it is due.

SECURED BONDS

Just as you have to put up collateral to get a loan, a company has to assure payment of a bond by offering some physical asset or property as collateral. This is called a *mortgage bond.* If the company is unable to repay the full face value of the bond at maturity, the bondholders can foreclose on the mortgage. They then assume ownership of the property and can sell it to pay off their bonds.

Corporations such as investment or finance companies that may themselves own securities of other companies may use some of these securities as collateral for the bonds *they* wish to sell. These are known as *collateral trust bonds.* If they are *in default,* that is the company can't pay at maturity, the securities are sold to make good on the debt.

In the railroad industry, bonds are frequently sold to finance the purchase of new rail cars. A trustee will arrange for the purchase of the cars and then, using the cars as collateral, will sell bonds to pay for them. These bonds are called *equipment trust certificates* or *bonds.*

These are all *secured bonds,* meaning that there is some form of collateral or tangible property that you, the lender—the bondholder—may take over if the company defaults on the debt.

DEBENTURES

A company that has exceptionally good credit may not have to offer any collateral with its bonds, just as you may be able to get a loan on no more than your signature and your promise to repay. These unsecured bonds are called *debentures.* The bondholders simply rely on the word of the company and the past history of the management that the bonds will be redeemed at full face value upon maturity.

Banks and institutions buy bonds with their depositors' or investors' money. You can appreciate why they would be reluctant to buy debentures, which offer no collateral. To get around this obstacle, a company may offer *sinking fund bonds.* These have no collateral but they require the company to set aside each year a specific sum of money that will total the full face value of the bonds at maturity.

CALLABLE AND CONVERTIBLE FEATURES

Your home mortgage may contain a clause that prevents you from paying off the debt within the first three or maybe five years without incurring a penalty. Bonds frequently have a similar clause—a *non-callable* provision—for a specified number of years.

Prevailing interest rates may be at 8 per cent when a bond is issued. A few years later interest rates may drop to 5 per cent on comparable new bonds. It is then profitable for the company to buy back—call—the 8 per cent bonds at face value and float a new issue with only a 5 per cent interest. If this happened, the company's gain would be your loss. Thus a *call feature* of a bond stipulates the conditions under which the bond may be redeemed by the issuer. It protects you by prohibiting the company from calling the bonds for a specified number of years.

A *convertible feature* makes a bond issue more attractive. It permits you to convert your $1,000 bond into a specified number of shares of common stock.

Assume that the common stock of a company is selling for $100 a share at the time your convertible bond is issued, and your bond can be converted *at any time* into ten shares of common stock. Simple arithmetic will show you that, because the bond is worth ten shares, if the price of the shares goes up to $110 your bond will be worth $1,100. Conversely, if the share price drops to $90 your bond will be worth only $900. Current interest rates also affect the price of convertible bonds as they do all other bonds.

BOND PRICES

Keep in mind that the amount of interest a bond pays stays constant year after year until maturity, or until it is called. Thus a 7 per cent bond will always pay $70 interest each year, regardless of how much other interest rates rise or fall.

If interest rates go up to 8 per cent, you could buy a new bond and receive $80 income each year on your investment. In deciding on a new purchase, you would avoid a 7 per cent bond, issued at an earlier time, that would pay you only $70 interest. The only way the 7 per cent bond would be attractive would be if you could buy it at a *discount,* that is, at less than $1,000. Thus, if you could buy the bond for only $875, the $70 interest would equal 8 per cent on your investment. The per cent yield is now the same for both bonds. Although you receive less income on one than on the other, you must realize that one costs you less than the other.

Percent Yield	×	*Cost of Bond*	=	*Dollar Income*
.08	×	$875	=	$70
.08	×	$1,000	=	$80

The same principle holds true in reverse. If interest rates drop to 6 per cent, the value of the 7 per cent bond would have to reach a level at which the $70 interest would equal the 6 per cent yield of new bonds. Thus, at a price of $1,166, the $70 interest would equal 6 per cent on your investment and be competitive with new bonds. You would then be buying the bond at a *premium.*

Percent Yield	×	*Cost of Bond*	=	*Dollar Income*
.06	×	$1,166	=	$70
.06	×	$1,000	=	$60

Both bonds have the same yield, and although one pays more, it also cost more.

As interest rates rise, the market value of the bonds you own goes down; as interest rates decline, the market value of your bonds rises. The only time current interest rates do not affect the price of your bonds is as they near maturity. Since the company is obliged to pay back only $1,000 for each bond at maturity, your bonds are worth only this face value in the few remaining months before they are redeemed.

If you buy or sell only one or two bonds, you will probably have to buy at a premium or sell at a discount from the quoted prices. It is much the same as the difference in the price per pound for a one-pound and a ten-pound bag of flour. With bonds there is less price variation when you trade in multiples of five and preferably ten at a time. This price variation is further aggravated by the fact that the bond market, which far exceeds *all* stock markets in security values, is dominated by large investors. The banks, insurance companies, retirement funds, etc., buy the majority of bonds in multiples of twenty-five and they may buy as many as a hundred or more of a single issue. Obviously, then, one or two bonds become a more costly transaction, paid for by a greater premium when you buy and a greater discount when you sell.

BOND RATINGS

If you lend a friend money, you have a pretty good idea whether or not he will repay the loan at the promised time. It's almost impossible for you and me to get this information when we want to lend a company money (buy a bond) without spending a great deal of time and effort. Fortunately we don't have to, because such independent agencies as Moody's and Standard & Poor's rate bonds as to the ability of companies to pay interest and principal—*face value*—as promised.

These ratings are AAA, AA, A, BBB, and so forth. The highest rating, that is, lowest risk, is AAA. You can appreciate that the greater the risk the higher the interest will have to be. Therefore an AAA bond will pay less interest than a BBB.

When you buy bonds for safety of principal, you are defeating your purpose if you buy one rated less than A. Always ask your broker or check Standard & Poor's *Bond Guide* for the rating of a bond you are considering. Don't rely on verbal assurances that "it's a safe investment with high interest." Find out the rating!

YIELD OR YIELD TO MATURITY

To figure out *current per cent yield* on a bond, divide the amount of interest paid each year by *current market value.* A bond paying $70 a year and selling at a discount for $875 would have a current yield of 8 per cent. 70.00÷875=.08. Current yield is satisfactory for most investment purposes—especially if you don't intend to hold the bond to maturity.

If you want to hold a bond to maturity, you may be offered two different bonds, each selling for $875 and paying $70 interest. The difference may be that one matures—is worth $1,000—in two years and the other in five years. Your $875 investment in either bond will increase by $125. In one case, though, it will be at a rate of $62.50 for each of the two years. In the other case it will be at the rate of $25 per year for each of five years. The two-year bond thus will earn $70 plus $62.50 for a total of $132.50 annually; the five-year bond will earn $70 plus $25 for a total of $95 annually. The *yield to maturity* is roughly figured by dividing this total annual amount by the current market value. The two-year bond has a yield to maturity of 132.50÷875=.1514 or 15.14 per cent and the five-year bond has a yield to maturity of 95.00÷875=.1085 or 10.85 per cent. The yield to maturity is used to evaluate the total return on your bond investment.

In this example the only difference between the bonds is the maturity dates. You can appreciate that if the two bonds also paid different rates of interest and were selling at different prices this would further complicate the comparison. Yield to maturity compensates for these variables and makes a comparison possible. You don't have to go through all this arithmetic. Your broker will do it for you precisely.

Government bonds

Government bonds are of three kinds: those issued by the federal government; those issued by political subdivisions, such as states, counties, towns—municipal bonds; and those issued by authorities, such as turnpike, bridge, tunnel, or port authorities. Like corporate bonds, these bonds are a contractual arrangement to borrow money for a specified length of time and rate of interest.

Just because you lend money to the federal government is no reason you shouldn't have assurance that your loan, a *government bond,* will pay regular interest and you will be paid back in full at maturity. Your assurance comes from Congress, which authorizes the Treasury not only to issue bonds but also to collect enough taxes to pay interest and principal. When you consider the tax capability of the Treasury, you need no further assurance that you will be paid. The money will be there and at the proper time. The money raised by the sale of these bonds is for general use and not earmarked for any particular project.

GOVERNMENT NOTES AND BILLS

In addition to bonds, the United States Treasury also sells *notes* and *bills.* The difference among them is the length of time between the date they are issued and the date they come due for payment. Bonds may not mature for twenty years. Notes mature in less than five years, bills in a matter of months.

Another difference is that the bonds and notes are originally sold at face value and interest is paid semi-annually. Bills, on the other hand, are sold at a *discount.* You lend $10,000 *less the amount of interest* and are repaid the full $10,000 when the loan comes due. Thus a thirty-day bill may cost you $9,850 and you are repaid $10,000. The difference of $150 is your interest.

Municipal bonds

States and political subdivisions are empowered by law to issue bonds. If they raise money for a general, not a specific, project the bonds are *general obligation bonds.* Interest and repayment of principal will come from the general tax revenue of the state or town issuing the bonds.

If your community undertakes a specific project, such as a new school, sewer, street construction, etc., but lacks the cash, it may float a special bond issue—say, Phoenixville Water and Sewer bonds. Interest and principal will be raised by a tax levy for that particular service.

AUTHORITY BONDS

An authority is a hybrid corporation operated by a branch of government that establishes it to build and operate facilities for the public. It is independent of any particular government body politic. A public transit company that serves a downtown area as well as surrounding suburbs operates in several political subdivisions, and each town is represented without political favoritism. Thus the Port of New York Authority is a facility operated for the benefit of an area spread over two states and several cities.

An authority is empowered to sell bonds to finance services and to levy tolls or charges for the use of the facilities. Fees are charged to cover operating costs and also to pay the interest and principal on the bonds. In most cases the sponsoring governments will guarantee interest and principal. But check these bonds carefully to see if the interest and principal are *guaranteed* or if they are simply a *moral* obligation of the sponsoring government. In the latter case, a different political party may be in office when interest comes due or the bonds mature. If the authority does not have the money to pay, there is no legal requirement for the sponsoring government to come to your rescue. A prime example was New York's Urban Development Corp. which in February of 1975 defaulted on more than $100 million of notes. If the state doesn't intervene in such a case, then there is little reason to expect the state to come to the rescue of the bondholders' investment of another $1.1 billion.

TAX-FREE BONDS

Pause before you rush out to buy government bonds because you have heard the interest is tax free. *Interest on bonds issued by the federal government is fully taxable. Only interest on municipal bonds, those issued by political subdivisions and authorities, is free of federal tax.*

These bonds may also be free of your state and local income taxes. Check with your broker or banker before buying them.

Take care also in buying out-of-state municipal bonds, expecting them to be free of your state and local income taxes. Your state may not recognize their tax-free status, because it wants you to invest in bonds issued in your home state.

To win your vote at campaign time, politicians stress the need to abolish tax-free bonds. They argue that the tax-free status of municipal bonds permits wealthy individuals to avoid paying income taxes. If the "loophole" is closed, they claim, the wealthy would have to pay their share and the rest of us would get an income tax reduction—or at least fewer tax increases. However, the fact is that tax-free bonds allow communities to make needed improvement at a lower cost to local taxpayers.

If your community needs $10 million dollars to build sewers, it could issue 8 per cent *taxable* bonds to finance the project. Then local taxes would have to raise $800,000 yearly just for interest. If the bond issue is tax free, a 5½ per cent—$550,000—interest might attract investors. This would save local taxpayers $250,000 a year. Politicians never mention this aspect and never contend that the government is in dire straits and needs this income tax revenue. They simply beguile the voter with specious arguments about making the wealthy pay and closing "loopholes."

For myself, I am most interested in keeping my own local taxes low. The sure way *not* to accomplish this is to succumb to the politicians' vote-getting appeal to abolish tax-free bonds.

WHO SHOULD BUY TAX-FREE BONDS?

Every *taxpayer* can benefit from tax-free bonds, but you benefit more if you are in a high income tax bracket. Suppose you are in a 40 per cent bracket and you receive taxable interest of $1,000; $400 income tax would be due and you would have $600 left to spend. If you are in a 25 per cent bracket, you would pay only $250 tax and have $750 left to spend. The higher your income tax bracket, therefore, the more profitable the tax-free bonds are for you.

However, if your income tax is less than 40 per cent of your taxable income, you will probably find that the extra income from taxable bonds is worth more to you than the saving on a tax-free bond. Check with your accountant or banker for your particular answer.

CHAPTER THREE

Mutual Funds

WHAT THEY CAN AND CANNOT DO FOR YOU

Mutual funds, like other forms of investments, have their times of great popularity followed by times of investor disenchantment. Basically, their attributes remain relatively constant. If they fulfill your investment requirements during popular times, then they no doubt will continue to do so during the periods of disenchantment on the part of other investors.

WHY MUTUALS?

Mutual funds meet two basic needs: *diversification* of your investments and *full-time management* of them. Women who are divorced or widowed or otherwise find themselves unexpectedly responsible for investments can especially appreciate this management need.

If you have less than $5,000 and invest in the stock of only one company, your portfolio is 100 per cent dependent on the price changes of that one security. On the other hand, if you invest your $5,000 equally in four different securities, then your portfolio is only 25 per cent dependent on the price changes of any one of them, and you have substantially reduced your risk.

Mutual funds permit you to spread your risk a great deal further. Your $5,000 is combined with the money from other investors, and the total, let's say, is a million dollars. This million-dollar portfolio can now be invested in an extremely wide selection of industries and a great many different companies. Should the price of any one of them decline, it will have only a slight effect on your $5,000 investment. At the same time, a mutual fund provides you with full-time management to achieve your specified objectives of growth, income, or some of both, for there are many types of mutuals.

CLOSED-END AND OPEN-END

Two basic types are: the closed-end and the open-end. When a *closed-end fund* is started, only a *specified number of shares* are issued at a specified offering price. Proceeds from this first sale are then invested by the new mutual fund and it commences operation. Later, if you want to buy shares, you must buy them from an owner of the fund's shares in the same way you would buy shares in any other company. If you want to sell shares, you must sell your shares to another investor who wants to buy shares in this same fund. Ordinarily shares of a closed-end fund are traded on one of the big exchanges and may be bought or sold through your broker.

The price of these closed-end fund shares fluctuates. It may be higher or lower than the share value of the fund's investments. It depends strictly on the supply and demand in the same way as do other stock prices. (See Chapter Eight, "Stock Exchanges.") The commission charged for buying and selling closed-end fund shares is the same as that charged for other stocks traded on the same exchange.

In contrast, the *open-end fund* starts with an offering of an unlimited—usually a minimum but no maximum—number of shares at a specific price. At the conclusion of the initial offering the proceeds are invested. From this point on, any number of shares in the fund may be bought from or sold back to the sponsor of the fund. There are continuous supply and demand. The fund determines the price of the shares by adding the total value of its investments and cash and subtracting any money owed. This total is then divided by the total number of shares owned by investors to arrive at a price or *net asset value* per share. The price, therefore, is determined by the fund's success in managing the investments. If investors buy more shares in the fund, there is more cash available for the fund to invest; if investors sell more shares, the fund may have to sell some of its investments so as to have the means of buying back investors' shares.

If you want to be assured that there will always be a buyer of your mutual fund shares, stick to the open-end fund because the fund stands ready to redeem them at any time. On the other hand if you feel certain that there will always be another investor willing to buy your fund shares, then a closed-end fund may meet your needs.

LOAD AND NO-LOAD FUNDS

Commissions for trading shares of an open-end fund vary widely but fall into two broad categories—the so-called load and no-load funds. The *load fund* is normally sold by brokers or fund salesmen and has a set commission rate or load. This is taken out of your purchase money. If you are investing $1,000 in an 8 per cent load fund priced at $10 per share, $80 would go for sales commissions; and the remaining $920 buys you ninety-two, not a hundred shares.

If you want to sell your shares back to the fund you may or may not be charged a "redemption fee." Some funds charge; some do not. These charges or commissions are stated in the literature or prospectus for each fund. *Do study this* carefully before you buy so you will know exactly what you must pay at the start.

The *no-load fund* is usually sold directly by the fund and not through a broker. A $1,000 investment buys a hundred shares at $10 each. Of course sales and promotion expenses are incurred just as with load funds, but they are less obvious since the no-load fund pays these expenses by deducting from income on the total investment, just as operating costs are usually paid.

Before you jump to the conclusion that only a fool would buy a load fund, consider that in both cases the cost of selling the shares to the public must somehow be paid by the fund. The difference is whether the cost is paid out of earnings *after* your investment is put to work or paid out *at the time* of your investment. There are valid arguments for each method. In any case *your decision on which mutual fund to buy should never be made solely on the basis of a load or no-load feature.*

There are many varieties of mutual funds, which range from conservative government bond funds to highly speculative stock funds. Conservative bond funds concentrate on safety of principal and good income; the speculative stock funds concentrate on growth of principal with greater risk and little or no income. As with other securities, it is impossible to combine maximum safety, maximum income, and maximum growth in the same investment. As your income and safety of principal increase, potential growth decreases; as your growth potential increases, your safety of income and principal decline.

Mutual funds, like life insurance, more often than not are *sold to you* rather than *bought by you.* The subtle difference is that a broker or salesman probably solicits your investment rather than your taking the initiative and shopping for it. This doesn't mean that you shouldn't be every bit as careful and selective when you buy a mutual fund as when you make any other investment. Mutual funds have well-defined objectives: income, growth, safety, or a moderate amount of each. The prospectus for each fund states what the objective is. If you have clearly defined your own investment objective, you have already determined which type of mutual fund you want to consider.

BOND FUNDS

Municipal bond funds carry the greatest safety because the face value of the bonds is guaranteed by whichever government body issues them. The money required to pay these bonds off at maturity, as well as to pay interest, is collected through some form of taxation. The possibility of the government not being able to redeem them at maturity is nil and the income may be tax free.

In the same general category are mutual bond funds that concentrate on corporate bonds—the bonds offered by business or industry. These funds may or may not have some municipal bonds in their portfolios. The risk in corporate bonds may be slightly greater but the income may also be higher.

Then there are funds made up of convertible corporate bonds and preferred stocks. Such portfolios are a safe conservative category and usually provide good income with more growth than the other two types of bond funds.

STOCK FUNDS

The majority of funds invest substantially in common stocks.

Their objective is generally to attain moderate income and growth with only a reasonable degree of risk. The percentages of their portfolios committed to common stocks, preferred stocks, and possibly bonds will usually determine whether their objective is oriented more toward growth or toward income. A *balanced fund*, as the name implies, invests in all three types of securities. It is geared to achieve reasonable income, some growth with modest risk, and relative safety of principal.

HEDGE FUNDS

Diametrically opposed to the bond funds from the standpoint of risk and income are the *hedge funds.* These are permitted all the latitude and discretion of an individual. Income is achieved more by accident than by design, since the hedge funds are oriented toward maximum growth. To achieve this, they may buy securities on margin, they may sell short, trade in options, and employ all the trading procedures the law allows. Hedge funds are for you only if you can afford substantially greater risk in pursuit of above-average growth of your investment.

DUAL-PURPOSE FUNDS

Between the extremes of bond funds and hedge funds there is the *dual-purpose fund.* This is the closed-end type and normally operates for a stated number of years, say seventeen. In this fund the total shares are divided equally between so-called *income* shares and so-called *capital* shares. You make your choice on the basis of your investment objective. Let's assume the first offering of the stock is for two million shares at $5.00 each—one million income shares and one million capital shares. Owners of the $5 million worth of income shares receive *all the income* from the total of $10 million invested. When the fund is terminated, owners of capital shares receive *all the capital gain* on the total $10 million.

If the total fund should yield 5 per cent, which is distributed only to the income-share owners, they would receive the equivalent of a 10 per cent return on their half of the fund. Similarly, if during the life of the fund it should appreciate 50 per cent, the amount distributed only to the capital-share owners would be equivalent to a 100 per cent appreciation on their half of the fund.

The dual-purpose fund can produce a high yield if you are looking for income or considerable growth if you are looking for gain without undue risk. But bear in mind two points about this type of fund: *if you invest for income, you don't participate in any gains or losses of principal; if you invest for capital gains, you receive no income.*

OTHER FUNDS

So long as there are managers of mutual funds, there will be new funds created to capitalize on current economic situations. In mid-1974 interest rates reached historic highs at the same time that the stock markets were sinking lower and lower. The average investor had many places to invest for a high rate of return, but the best were out of reach because of the large minimum cash required. It wasn't long before mutual funds were started that permitted the small investor to participate.

Municipal bond funds were started that invested solely in long-term bonds the income from which would be free of federal income taxes. The small investor, who might on her own be able to buy only three or four such tax-free bonds at a premium, was given the opportunity to diversify and avoid the premium. In addition, full-time professional management was provided.

For those who wanted to capitalize on the highest rates of interest without regard to tax consequences, Money Market funds were started. These restrict their investments to such securities as top-quality commercial paper, banker's acceptances, U.S. government securities, certificates of deposit, and the like. As an individual you could buy these same securities, but to attain the high rate of return, your investment would be tied up for a specific length of time. Investing in the fund, however, permits you to sell at any time *with no loss of return.*

YOUR FRIEND THE STOCK GUIDE

Before you make any decisions, ask your broker for a copy of the *Stock Guide* published by Standard & Poor's Corporation. At the back you will find a detailed listing of open-end mutual funds with a wealth of information—not the least of which is the investment objective of each.

Out of 400 or so funds listed, you can select those having the same investment objective that you have—whether it is G (growth), I (income) or S (safety of principal). (See Figure 1.) Some funds list only one objective while others list two or three in order of importance to the fund, as GIS. If you have a single objective, then you can eliminate all those with multiple objectives, as well as those with objectives different from yours. If you have a priority of objectives, such as GI, you can eliminate those funds that do not have the same order of priority, such as IG.

Notice that the name of each fund is followed by the year in which it was formed. You may have a preference for organizations whose performance can be investigated over a period of years through all types of market and economic conditions. Or you may prefer a newer fund on the basis that it must perform better if it is to become established. There are good arguments for old and new funds, and therefore it must be your own choice. You can now eliminate more funds from your list; those that do not fulfill your requirement for length of operation.

You may also have a preference for a large mutual fund over a small one or vice versa. The fourth column shows the total net assets in millions of dollars for each fund; assets range from less than a million dollars on upward. If size is important to you, your list can be further reduced. On this point, too, strong arguments can be made for large, medium, or small mutual funds; so, again, these requirements should be viewed as your personal preference.

Your list of possible mutual funds will now be only a fraction of the four hundred or so listed in the *Guide*, and it is of a size to let you investigate performance in greater detail. But bear in mind that you are looking at *past performance*. There is no assurance that the funds will perform as well, better, or worse in the future. However, there is a good possibility that, relative to the general market and economic conditions, their performance will not change radically.

If you are content to check a mutual fund's performance *over a period of four years*, the information is in the *Guide*. If you

Fund	Year Formed	Prin. Obj.	Type	Dec. 31, 1974 Total Net Assets (Mil.$)	Cash & Equiv (Mil.$)	See Foot-notes	Net Assets per Share % Change from Previous Dec. 31 At: Dec. 31 1971	1972	1973	1974	Jan. 31 1975	Min. Unit	Max. Sales Chg. %	Distributions per Share from Invest. Income 1974	1975	Security Profits 1974	1975	PRICE RECORD NAV Per Sh 11-Yr Range 1964-1974 High	Low	—1975— High	Low	#1-31-75 NAV Per Shr.	Offer Price	% Yield From Inv. Inc.
Composite Fund	'49	GI	C	27.8	10.5	.....	+ 6.8	+ 0.9	− 29.0	− 15.9	+ 11.6	$500	8.7	0.28	0.07	....	....	13.57	5.16	6.26	5.61	6.26	6.80	4.1
Comstock	'68	G	C	45.3	6.7	.....	+ 8.2	− 3.0	− 18.2	− 18.8	+ 19.6	$50	8.5	0.08	....	....	....	6.51	2.48	3.36	2.80	3.35	3.66	2.2
Constellation Growth	'67	G	L	3.0	0.0	.....	+ 1.7	+ 5.8	− 16.3	− 27.5	+ 11.9	$250	None	0.06	....	....	....	14.78	3.61	4.38	3.88	4.34	4.34	1.4
Consultant's Mutual Inv	'63	GI	B	7.9	2.5	ʃ	+ 15.1	+ 5.3	− 19.8	− 20.9	+ 4.8	$500	None	0.38	0.16	....	....	16.63	8.10	9.28	8.92	9.18	9.18	4.1
Contrafund	'67	G	C	18.0	0.1	§	+ 6.0	+ 14.6	− 11.9	− 16.0	+ 7.8	....	None	0.22	....	0.27	....	14.78	6.16	7.84	7.21	7.77	....	2.1
Corporate Leaders Tr B	'54	SIG	C	36.4	0.7	1	+ 10.7	+ 14.4	− 17.2	− 31.5	+ 15.3	$500	8.31	0.949	....	....	....	19.34	9.47	11.71	10.03	11.56	12.74	7.4
Country Capital Invest	*'66	G	C	27.0	8.2	.....	+ 25.3	+ 10.3	− 21.0	− 26.4	+ 6.5	$100	7.5	0.37	....	....	....	17.59	7.93	9.46	8.86	9.44	10.21	3.6
Crown Western:																								
Diversified Fd.	'45	I	B	9.6	1.7	.....	+ 7.8	+ 4.7	− 18.0	− 17.8	+ 4.3	$20	8.5	0.289	0.154	....	....	9.91	3.96	4.61	4.34	4.57	4.99	5.8
Dallas Fd.	'54	G	C	3.6	1.1	.....	+ 17.8	+ 9.2	− 29.6	− 18.2	+ 4.5	$20	8.5	0.139	0.083	....	....	17.64	3.97	4.93	4.54	4.87	5.32	2.6
Davidge Early Bird	*'69	G	H	1.3	0.5	.....	+ 45.6	+ 6.2	− 56.3	− 31.3	+ 12.8	None	None	0.035	....	....	....	19.01	4.48	5.22	4.62	5.21	5.21	0.7
De Vegh Mutual	'50	G	C	61.7	11.5	.....	+ 17.4	− 0.9	− 19.7	− 22.9	+ 10.1	$500	None	1.31	....	....	....	84.66	40.68	49.17	44.48	48.99	48.99	2.7
Decatur Income	'56	I	C	187.9	9.0	.....	+ 11.0	+ 0.5	− 19.2	− 18.2	+ 11.7	1sh.	8.5	0.65	0.15	....	....	15.60	7.01	8.50	7.59	8.48	9.27	7.0
Delaware Fund	'37	GI	C	276.0	23.2	.....	+ 12.3	+ 4.6	− 28.1	− 20.5	+ 12.2	1sh.	8.5	0.40	....	....	....	18.25	6.39	7.84	6.99	7.84	8.57	4.7
Delta Trend	'68	G	C	7.2	0.2	.....	+ 19.7	− 7.9	− 33.8	− 38.7	+ 11.6	1sh.	8.5	0.05	....	....	....	10.09	2.57	3.27	2.93	3.27	3.57	1.4
Directors Capital	'70	G	C	3.8	1.4	.....	+ 31.6	+ 11.3	− 27.9	− 24.9	+ 0.3	$250	8.75	....	0.186	....	....	8.54	2.85	3.21	3.05	3.06	3.35	...
Dividend Shares	'32	IG	C	235.2	16.5	.....	+ 9.2	+ 12.5	− 16.6	− 26.2	+ 11.3	$500	8.67	0.125	0.025	0.11	....	4.23	2.05	2.58	2.31	2.57	2.81	4.4
Dodge & Cox Balanced	'31	ISG	B	10.9	0.5	ʃ	+ 7.0	+ 7.7	− 13.1	− 25.6	+ 4.6	$250	None	0.94	....	0.19	....	28.11	14.40	16.40	15.83	16.35	16.35	5.7
Dodge & Cox Stock	'64	GI	C	8.6	0.3	.....	+ 13.0	+ 10.2	− 14.7	− 27.7	+ 12.6	$250	None	0.51	....	....	....	19.26	5.07	11.99	10.65	11.99	11.99	4.3
Drexel Equity	'61	G	C	12.3	3.3	.....	+ 12.2	− 1.3	− 37.3	− 20.0	+ 10.3	$250	None	....	0.38	....	....	22.11	6.52	7.80	7.07	7.80	7.80	...
Dreyfus Fund	'47	GIS	C	1209.8	43.2	.....	+ 10.5	+ 5.0	− 19.6	− 22.0	+ 7.2	$25	8.75	0.25	0.15	....	....	16.90	7.15	8.83	8.24	8.83	9.68	2.6
Dreyfus Group Equity	*'72	GIS	C	1.6	0.6	.....	....	....	− 25.6	− 18.7	+ 6.5	$10	3.0	0.083	....	....	....	5.28	2.95	3.30	3.05	3.29	3.52	2.4
Dreyfus Leverage	'68	GIS	C	203.1	46.6	.....	+ 28.6	+ 11.1	− 15.4	− 28.1	+ 4.0	$500	8.75	0.275	....	....	....	19.01	9.54	10.87	10.41	10.86	11.90	2.3
Dreyfus Spec Inc.	*'72	IGS	BD	44.0	6.6	.....	....	− 0.2	− 12.8	− 17.3	+ 8.1	$500	8.75	0.505	....	....	....	8.59	5.59	6.40	5.92	6.40	7.01	7.2
Dreyfus Third Century	*'72	GIS	C	13.2	1.0	.....	....	− 9.9	− 12.3	− 30.8	+ 17.3	$500	8.75	0.15	....	....	....	11.56	....	8.02	6.84	8.02	8.79	1.7
E&E Mutual	'57	GIS	C	n/a	n/a	.....	+ 21.2	+ 18.1	− 18.0	− 21.6	+ 10.3	$100	None	0.04	....	....	....	8.67	1.89	2.68	2.43	2.68	2.68	1.5
Eagle Growth	*'71	GI	C	1.9	0.1	.....	....	+ 8.7	− 24.4	− 25.0	+ 13.5	$150	8.75	0.17	....	....	....	10.69	5.00	6.01	5.27	5.98	6.55	2.6
Eaton & Howard:																								
Balanced	'32	GIS	B	102.9	5.8	.....	+ 6.6	+ 10.0	− 7.6	− 23.1	+ 5.5	None	8.5	0.417	0.113	0.35	....	13.96	6.15	7.36	6.93	7.34	8.02	5.2
Growth	*'68	G	C	22.7	5.2	.....	+ 25.3	+ 23.2	− 32.7	− 44.8	+ 13.9	None	8.5	0.04	0.08	0.20	....	18.88	5.52	7.13	6.26	7.13	7.79	0.5
Income	'32	I	BD-C	24.1	3.1	.....	+ 12.4	+ 2.8	− 8.3	− 17.3	+ 6.3	None	8.5	0.434	0.12	0.112	....	8.49	4.58	5.21	4.85	5.21	5.69	7.6
Special	'67	G	C	12.3	3.8	.....	+ 25.7	+ 3.4	− 32.3	− 41.1	+ 12.0	None	8.5	0.035	0.102	....	....	17.29	3.97	4.59	4.10	4.59	5.02	0.7
Stock	'31	SGI	C	109.7	14.3	.....	+ 10.4	+ 11.9	− 18.5	− 34.8	+ 7.5	None	8.5	0.307	0.09	0.305	....	18.91	6.25	7.95	7.34	7.93	8.67	3.5
Edie Spec. Growth	'69	G	C	21.4	3.2	.....	+ 33.3	+ 15.9	− 41.0	− 33.5	+ 18.9	$1,000	None	0.25	....	....	....	32.16	11.11	13.96	11.74	13.96	13.96	1.8
Edie Spec. Instit.	'69	G	C	16.9	2.9	ʃ	+ 34.0	+ 15.1	− 39.3	− 37.7	+ 7.0	$1,000	None	0.90	....	....	....	80.33	27.81	31.45	29.94	31.45	31.45	2.9
Egret Fund	'64	R	C	30.9	4.0	2	+ 11.9	+ 11.5	− 21.0	− 30.0	+ 5.6	$100	8.0	0.30	....	....	....	16.50	7.43	8.62	8.12	8.62	9.37	3.2
Emerging Securities	'68	G	C	2.2	0.4	.....	+ 13.4	+ 0.7	− 50.1	− 27.5	0.0	....	None	....	....	....	....	9.67	2.19	2.19	2.19	2.19	2.19	...
Energy	'52	G	SP	110.8	18.1	.....	+ 6.0	+ 9.0	− 8.8	− 22.1	+ 8.8	10sh.	None	0.40	....	....	....	17.65	8.00	9.91	9.11	9.91	9.91	4.0

Uniform Footnote Explanations—See end of alphabet. **Stock Splits & Divs.** (figures adjusted): [1]Incl. return of cap.:$0.324'72,$0.04'73,$0.33'74. [2]$200 Yearly min.purch.

1. Standard & Poor's Mutual Fund Record

want to check performance over a longer period, *Barron's National Business and Financial Weekly* (on most newsstands) includes every three months a "Quarterly Mutual Fund Record." This gives statistics over a ten-year period. Wiesenberger Services, Inc. (your broker can lend you a copy), publishes facts and figures on all funds for their entire term of operation.

Of course you may feel that, because this is historical data and you are investing for the future, data on *recent* performance is adequate. The two chief advantages to the longer history are that, first, you can relate performance to market conditions over the years and, second, you can get some idea of how consistent management has been even though personnel may have changed substantially during a ten-year period. Whichever your choice, these facts are available: the year-to-year per cent change in net assets per share; payments to shareholders from the fund's dividend income; payments from capital gains, etc. On the basis of this information, your list of mutual funds will probably be down to only a few names.

On the load funds, your broker can furnish you with literature, and no doubt he can also help you obtain literature on the no-load funds that are sold direct by the mutual funds.

MORE THAN ONE FUND?

In the course of time there is a tendency to buy shares in more than one fund, the result of having cash available or perhaps an inheritance at a time when a fund salesman solicits your investment. At such a time, keep in mind that the purpose of a mutual fund is (1) diversification and (2) professional management for a stated objective. Owning shares in a second or third mutual fund merely duplicates, with the disadvantage of more record keeping, tax reporting, etc. However, if your reason for wanting to buy a second mutual fund with additional cash is that you are not completely satisfied with the performance of your first fund, then sell the first fund and put all your money in the second.

WHAT TO COMPARE

Most mutual funds include in their literature either a graph or a chart showing a substantial increase in value of a hypothetical investment over a certain number of years. It is impressive when you observe that $10,000 invested ten years earlier has multiplied many times over. Your thoughts immediately turn to the investments you may have made over these years and you find it difficult to recall even one of your stocks that has performed with anywhere near this success. At this point you may conclude that the mutual fund is a far superior method of investing. Before you sell your own investing capabilities short, though, consider certain factors.

Possibly you are comparing individual securities in your portfolio with the *total* performance of the fund. Doubtless the fund has had its share of losers, but they were offset by winners in the portfolio. Your total portfolio may be just as good as the fund's.

Also, the chart of the mutual fund usually has a footnote to the effect that the figures assume that all dividends and capital gains were reinvested in the fund. Chances are that when you received dividends on your other investments during the same ten-year period, you spent them on something other than more securities—even small dividends can add up substantially over a ten-year period. And if you realized capital gains, you may have held out enough to pay the capital gains tax. The fund, on the other hand, assumes total reinvestment and the tax is not considered. If your own portfolio were plotted on the same basis as the mutual fund, your performance would doubtless be substantially better than what comes to mind when you first look at the charts of the fund.

These performance charts are not really misleading when you understand why they include reinvestment of capital gains and dividends and no taxes on profits. On the assumption that you will be comparing the performance of several funds that may have different objectives, each fund includes in its figures everything that contributes to total performance. Taxes, which vary from one individual to another, are excluded. In this way you may accurately compare the *total performance* of a growth fund, with little income, to an income fund, with little growth. The point is, compare mutual fund charts with one another and not with your own investments. Considering the same factors, your portfolio may have outperformed the funds over the same period of time.

EARNINGS AND TAXES

Most mutual funds provide the investor with two options. *Dividends* earned by the fund's investments may be paid in cash or they may be reinvested through the purchase of additional shares. *Capital gains* realized by a fund may also be paid in cash or reinvested in shares of the fund. Regardless of your choice, at the end of the year you will receive a statement showing the dividends, interest, and/or capital gains you received. *These must be declared on your tax return and the applicable taxes paid even if they were reinvested.*

The fact that you pay capital gains taxes on them annually is a seldom noted advantage of mutual funds. Should you wish to turn in your shares, a substantial portion of the taxes on their appreciation would already have been paid on an annual basis up to the current year. Compare this with the sale of a ten-year investment in IBM or Eastman Kodak, which may have quadrupled in value. On such a sale, the entire capital gains taxes must be paid in one fell swoop. Considering that taxes are likely to go up in the future, paying them at today's rates may cost you less than later.

In some cases a mutual fund may provide you with a third option—switching from one fund to another. Perhaps your objective at first is growth; subsequently, owing to changed financial circumstances, you may require greater income. Some managements operate several mutual funds, each with a different objective, and they will permit you to exchange shares of one of their funds for another at a minimal charge or none at all. This is a desirable feature, but it certainly does not take precedence over the ability of the fund to achieve its stated objective.

In essence, the mutual fund provides the small investor, the uninformed, or the investor who does not wish to handle the business herself with diversification and professional management for a stated objective. If you are a non-saver, it can help you put money aside regularly through the optional reinvestment of your dividends and capital gains. Although you should always keep some money in a savings account for emergencies, your excess money can do more for you in a well-managed mutual fund. But be sure to select a mutual fund as carefully as any other security, and regard it as a long-term investment that still requires periodic checking on its performance.

CHAPTER FOUR

Banking Your Money

SAVINGS ACCOUNTS AREN'T THE ONLY WAY

Wise management does not mean keeping fully invested in stocks and bonds. There will be times when you sell a security before deciding on a good replacement or you may want to sit on the side lines, particularly if the market seems to be going down. Rather than leave the cash in your checking account where you may be tempted to spend it and where it isn't earning any interest, you will want to put it to work.

How you do this depends on how long you want to stay out of the market and how much extra cash you have.

SAVINGS ACCOUNTS

Your local savings bank or savings and loan association is the most readily available depository for your excess cash, and these institutions require only a small minimum deposit. A savings account offers the benefit of being insured up to $40,000, so your nest egg is well protected. If you have more than $40,000, you can open a second account in the same bank under another name, as Mrs. M. L. Smith instead of simply Mary L. Smith, or you can go to another bank. Just be sure that your funds earn interest from the day of deposit to the day of withdrawal.

Of course you realize that, in return for safety and the privilege of being able to withdraw your money on short notice, you will not be earning the maximum interest you can get elsewhere.

SAVINGS CERTIFICATES AND CERTIFICATES OF DEPOSIT

At the present time you can increase the amount of interest if you are willing to leave your money deposited for a certain length of time. Savings banks offer Certificates of Deposit (C.D.s). In essence you guarantee that you won't withdraw your cash for a specified period of time. Certificates are usually available for as little as $1,000 for one year, and you can earn an extra half per cent or more for each additional year you let your money remain. Of course this premium interest is greater for a $10,000, $50,000, or $100,000 certificate of deposit and increases still more for a two-year or five-year certificate.

Your money is safe in such an investment, and in a real emergency can be withdrawn, although you will then lose the premium part of the interest. While your money is working for you in a bank, you are relieved of making any investment decisions until the time period is up.

To take advantage of the higher interest rates offered by large denominations of C.D.s, pools have been formed with several participants, each contributing $10,000 or $20,000, and each receiving a part ownership of a $100,000 certificate. Aside from questions of legality, such an arrangement opens the door to many possible complications. What happens to the arrangement if one participant dies? What happens to your estate if you die? What happens if there is a falling out among the partners? I haven't even bothered to find answers to such questions because the extra yield isn't worth that kind of aggravation to you. There are better ways to increase yield.

COMMERCIAL PAPER

For the larger portfolio, there is Commercial Paper. This constitutes a short-term loan to a corporation and requires a minimum of $25,000. It is a loan strictly on the promise of repayment by a corporation. Therefore the risk is judged solely on the integrity of the company. The interest rate varies accordingly but is usually higher than may be had in a savings account or certificate of deposit.

My preference is for quality Thirty-Day Paper. This is available through your broker at a nominal service charge. By the end of thirty days a suitable stock may have been selected or the trend of the market in general may be improved and the money can be reinvested. If such isn't the case, the paper may be "rolled over" (the loan continued) with a good rate of return.

Brokers aren't anxious for this business because the service charge is only $20 or so, which is substantially less than the commission on the purchase of stock worth $25,000. However, they prefer Commercial Paper when they know your alternative is a savings account. Furthermore, when the paper comes due, the broker collects for you and has an opportunity to earn a commission if you then decide to go into the market again.

TREASURY BILLS

If you don't care for the risk factor of Commercial Paper, have less cash available, and are willing to wait somewhat longer, you can buy Treasury bills. These are I.O.U.s of the United States Treasury. They are available in minimum denominations of $10,000 with maturities of three, six, or twelve months. These bills are auctioned every Monday by the Federal Reserve Bank. Although you can submit your bid direct, you will find it easier to buy through your banker or broker for a small service charge. If you want to buy direct, the Federal Reserve Bank in your district will send you a detailed pamphlet explaining the procedure.

The interest rate will be a bit lower than from Commercial Paper, but this is what you sacrifice for the greater degree of safety.

TREASURY BONDS

As a part of your savings for a rainy day, you would do well to consider Treasury bonds. These represent long-term loans to the United States Treasury and are available in denominations of $1,000. Like other bonds, they are bought and sold regularly by investors and almost all sell at a discount. As a result, you don't have to have a great deal of money to buy them. Although you take a chance that the market value may decline, the redemption *at maturity* is guaranteed by the government.

Some issues of Treasury bonds are known variously as

"flower" or "tombstone" bonds. These particular issues have an extra feature that permits their use *at full face value* for payment of federal inheritance taxes. The bonds need not be held a specified length of time, perhaps only a few hours, so long as they are *owned* by the deceased at the time of death. They cannot be bought by an estate to pay taxes. Since none of us has a choice of when a fatal accident or death from natural causes may occur, I recommend them for people of all ages who have substantial assets. After all, if a $1,000 estate tax can be paid with a bond that cost $800, there is that much more for the heirs.

Any of these banking plans that tie up your money for a moderate length of time and meanwhile earn a reasonable rate of return will help your approach to good investing. The psychological urgency to rush out pell-mell and buy stocks is removed. You can calmly consider your next move and which stocks look as if they will do well over the longer term. A friend's hot tip or your broker's urgent recommendation can be considered more rationally. Banking your money can indeed be profitable.

CHAPTER FIVE

What Do You Want Most?

INCOME, GROWTH, OR BOTH IN MODERATION

Your success in investing your money, no matter how you choose to do it, can best be determined in only one way—how close your investments come to achieving *your objectives.* Therefore, until you establish your objectives, you can't say for sure whether or not you are investing successfully. (See Chapter Fourteen, "The Quarterly Checkup.")

You are the only one who can accurately determine your needs. It's like decorating a room—the result may not suit someone else, but if it's what you want or need, then you have been successful. Just as you can't decorate a formal living room to double as a recreation room, you can't invest for maximum income and expect also to have maximum growth. A portfolio of bonds will provide maximum income with little growth and a portfolio of stocks will provide less income but more growth. Right at the start you have to decide whether you want your portfolio to grow or produce income or give you a reasonable amount of both. *Then stick to your objective.*

Of course your objective is based on your financial needs as they exist now. If a major change occurs—retirement, long-term illness, children's education, etc.—then you may have to change your investment objective and consequently the securities in your portfolio. The point is not to change unless you have to, and then to maintain the new objective.

INVESTING FOR INCOME

The term "investing for income" is fine as a generality. In actual practice you have to define exactly what you mean. To one person it may mean 4 per cent yield and to another 8 per cent yield. This makes a lot of difference in the securities you buy.

First decide on the approximate *dollar income* you would like your portfolio to provide. Divide this figure by the value of your portfolio, and you will have the *per cent yield.* If you need $1,000 income and your investments are worth $20,000, then you are looking for securities that will give you a 5 per cent yield: 20,000÷1,000=.05, or 5 per cent. Now you have a specific yield requirement that your investments must meet. Not only will this provide facts to give your broker, but you can avoid a lot of well-intentioned suggestions from outsiders and friends. Your investment decisions *based on facts* will make you considerably more confident than decisions *based on fancy.*

If you are investing for maximum income, in all probability you can't afford a great deal of risk. Fortunately the securities providing good income, bonds, have minimal risk of falling in value, but you also have to understand that they don't stand as good a chance for appreciation as stocks.

The best and most secure income is provided by quality corporate bonds that may yield 8 per cent compared to common stocks that are yielding 3 to 4 per cent. Although the price of bonds may fluctuate, they will be worth neither more nor less than their face value when they are ultimately redeemed.

If you can afford a slightly lower yield and a little more risk, investigate utility stocks. The preferred issues will yield a little more than the common. Both offer a higher return than most other industry stocks—Detroit Edison currently yields 13 per cent while Exxon yields 7 per cent. In exchange for the slightly lower yield than on bonds, utility stocks generally fluctuate more in value. So in addition to good income you also stand a chance of getting some appreciation in the value of your securities.

Next in order of income producers are the common stocks of corporations. In this category there is a wide range of yields varying with the profitability of the companies. You may well find the stock with the income you need, but check with your broker and determine that the *dividend is fairly secure.* Dividends are paid from profits, and dividends may not be paid if profits disappear. A couple of good examples are White Motor Company in 1970 and Great Atlantic & Pacific Tea Company in 1972. In both cases you could have bought the stock in anticipation of a 5 per cent or greater yield, at the time exceptionally good, only to find suddenly that the dividends were omitted because profits had declined.

The fact is that if you determine your income needs you and your broker have something tangible on which to base your investment decisions.

INVESTING FOR GROWTH

This is another term to be defined when you move from friendly discussion to serious broker consultation. Keep in mind that the greater the potential for rapid growth the greater the risk for precipitous decline.

The price of Eastman Kodak stock has appreciated about 15 per cent compounded annually for the twelve years ending in mid-1973 compared to almost double that rate for Polaroid. Both are considered growth stocks and yield about 1 per cent. From mid-1973 to the end of 1974, while the stock market declined some 45 per cent, Kodak lost about 55 per cent in value and Polaroid about 85 per cent. In each case the price recovered, but over a period of years, Polaroid with its greater growth has had more and wider price fluctuations than the slightly slower growth Kodak. The point is that, since you never know when a catastrophe will use up your savings account and also take some of your investments, you may be better off with slightly slower- and steadier-growing stocks. This is a decision only you can make.

The following figures will give you an idea of annual growth rates translated into profit after five years.

5%	growth each year for five years =	27% total gain
10%	" " " " " " =	60% total gain
15%	" " " " " " =	100% total gain
20%	" " " " " " =	150% total gain
25%	" " " " " " =	200% total gain

If your definition of growth is to double your money in five years, you can look for a stock with a growth potential of 15 per cent each year. If you are trying to triple your investment in five years—200 per cent profit—you will have to ask your broker for stocks capable of growing steadily at a rate of 25 per cent each year. These figures indicate how much annual appreciation to look for when you give your broker specific targets.

The one thing high-growth stocks have in common is low yield. Good ones may be found in a wide range of industries and not just in the highly publicized Walt Disney, IBM, and Xerox. Here are some whose price has grown at an annual rate of more than 15 per cent over the twelve years from 1962 to 1974.

Amp, Inc.	Electrical devices
Delta Airlines	Air transport
Eckerd Corporation	Drugstores
International Flavors & Fragrances	Extracts and concentrates
Johnson & Johnson	Surgical dressings
Masco Corporation	Faucets
Quaker State Oil & Refining	Petroleum

The principal feature to look for is a *record of sustained price appreciation* that looks as if it can be maintained, rather than just a flash-in-the-pan appreciation during the past year or so. Securities Research Company published *Cycli-Graphs*, which charts the price, dividends, and earnings of more than one thousand stocks over the past twelve years. You will find it helpful in discovering these growth stocks.

THE HAPPY MEDIUM

Somewhere between investing solely for maximum income or solely for maximum growth there is a happy medium that will provide you with moderate income and reasonable growth. Here too *you* have to decide *what you are looking for* and your starting point again is the required income figure. Once this yield is established, you or your broker can start your search for the stock that may also give you satisfactory growth. (See Chapter Eleven, "Evaluating Stocks.")

MIDDLE-OF-THE-ROAD SECURITIES

With more than two thousand securities listed on the New York and American Stock exchanges and hundreds more traded over the counter, you have a wide selection that can come close to your investment objectives and make up your portfolio. Later, if one no longer meets your requirements, sell it and switch to another.

Some investors split their portfolios, investing half in high-income securities and half in high-growth. The intent is for the *whole portfolio* to produce moderate income and moderate growth. Going back to our recreation-room, living-room analogy, mixing French provincial furniture, wall tapestries, and crystal fixtures with indoor-outdoor carpeting, folding chairs, and a pool table only gives you a mishmash. Each item may be perfect alone but, combined, each detracts from the other. With all semiformal furnishings, the same room becomes an attractive semiformal family room.

This concept of mixing high-income and high-growth securities is pushed by many professionals. I suspect there is a better chance of commissions than there is with middle-of-the-road securities you may hold for quite some time.

PART TWO

The People Who Work for Your Investments

CHAPTER SIX

How to Select a Broker

BE VERY PARTICULAR

I am told that when a woman moves to another town or city one of her major concerns is locating a new hairdresser who will fix her hair the way she wants it. Apparently doctors and dentists are easy to find, but putting a finger on a suitable hairdresser is no simple matter. So there are consultations. If the coiffeurs of some friends look attractive, that of another awful, investigations are made and trial appointments set up, usually with more than one beauty parlor. Selecting a broker should be managed even more carefully. Find out whom your investing friends are using, whether they are satisfied with results, and particularly whether their objectives are about the same as yours; that is, whether they are looking for *growth* or *income* or *some of each.*

Actually your broker is worth a lot of investigation, for he is to render you important services. He is going to recommend stocks and bonds and handle your money. You must be able to work confidently with him and respect his ability. On the other hand, remember that the *money* you have to invest is *yours* and it is your responsibility to see that it is handled properly. A good broker can help you, and you want to be sure that that's just what he is, good, and good for you.

WHAT TO EXPECT FROM YOUR BROKER

Before you start looking for a broker, know what to expect from him and also just what assistance you need to manage your investments. Your broker was hired by his firm for his sales ability, not because he had a knack for picking good investments. Selecting investments is the function of other people in the firm. The broker is the one who relays selections to you.

Keep in mind that the firm—and in many cases your broker—operate on commissions earned from both buying and selling securities. It's up to your broker to persuade you to buy and sell—trade—with his firm. Consider your broker, therefore, in the same light as any other salesman with whom you deal. He must:

Understand your circumstances
Know your investment objectives
Give you factual information
Give you service
Let you make your own decisions
Be efficient

You may have other requirements for the broker you want, but be sure to establish in your mind what you are looking for before starting the search.

SELECT, DON'T SETTLE

I work with brokers who have become friends, but I never work with a broker because he is a friend. In other words, the selection is first on ability as a broker, not on the basis of any social relationship. In this way, if I become dissatisfied with his service I am free to take my business elsewhere with fewer hurt feelings.

Too often convenience is a deciding factor. If there is only one broker in town you may resign yourself to doing business with him. Then you may feel trapped and stuck with his service regardless of quality. Actually brokers advertise far and wide, and those at a distance would also gladly accept your business. So there's no reason not to take time to look in nearby towns for a good broker. Chances are that most of your contacts with him will be by phone or mail anyway and, since most firms accept collect calls, it costs you nothing to have a broker at a distance.

The same applies if you already have a good broker but must move away. Take him with you—at least temporarily—via long-distance telephone and mail.

WHERE TO START

First spend some time investigating. Check with friends who you know invest. Find out what firms and what brokers handle their business. As you talk, it will be obvious which friends are conservative and which are speculative investors. *The recommendations of those with objectives similar to yours should be given first consideration.* The broker who does an excellent job providing good income for one client may do a poor job providing growth for another.

Check also with the trust officer at your bank. He will be familiar with many brokers and be interested in giving you, a bank customer, good information. You will probably find that one or two firms are mentioned more often than others. These are the firms to investigate further.

MEET THE MANAGER

Too often investors learn too late that their "mutual understanding" with their broker was all one way. The problem stems from the broker's asking the client about her bank balance, her marital status, and many other "prying" questions, but the client rarely asks the broker pertinent questions. A certain aura of mutual trust also develops because brokers accept telephone orders for large sums without asking for any down payments or cash in advance. Don't kid yourself! This isn't trust, the *law* requires transactions to be paid for within five days, and it's the law the brokers trust, not you. Your trust in the broker should develop first on the basis of *your* prying questions, not just a sense of trust.

When you talk to the firm's manager, tell him that you are *thinking* of opening an account and let him know your investment objectives—you want *all growth, all income, or a reasonable amount of each.* Tell him also approximately the amount you wish to invest.

Always remember that it is *your money* and *you are the customer*. Make the manager convince—sell—you on the fact that his firm will do a good job for you. If he can't convince you, don't waste any more time; go to the next firm on your list.

MEET YOUR BROKER

Once a manager has sold you on doing business with his firm he will introduce you to your broker—a registered representative. Of course, if you have the name of an individual, ask to meet him also.

Understand that a registered representative has passed an examination required by the Securities and Exchange Commission (S.E.C.) that qualifies him to buy, sell, and answer investment questions for clients. Upon passing the exam, he or she is registered with the S.E.C. and is variously referred to as an account executive, customer's man, or broker. Calling him an "account executive" is like referring to a housekeeper as a residential manager. Brokers are simply *salesmen* whose product is service.

Tell your broker what you told the manager—how much you wish to invest and your objective. Then let him sell you, convince you that he can make suitable recommendations and give you good service. Here are some of the questions you should get him to answer:

> What profitable recommendations has he made for his clients? He'll tell about these without prompting.
>
> Has he recently made some bad recommendations? If his answer is no, you can't trust him.
>
> How bad were his losses? Everyone can make a bad investment, but the reliable broker *admits the mistake* and doesn't hesitate to *advise the investor to sell.*
>
> What bonds have his customers bought? If he is negative about bonds, it may be that he is more interested in *higher commissions* from trading stocks than in what's best for his client's portfolio.
>
> Does he ever recommend "short sales"? (See Chapter Seven, "How to Work with Your Broker.") If he does, he may be more speculative than you care for.
>
> Does he ever advise clients to keep reserves of cash? If so, it denotes conservatism, and clients were well advised.

> How long has he been a broker? You want someone who has experienced both rising and falling markets, not a youngster new at the business.

You may have qualms about asking questions like these, but *you have a right to know* on what grounds—other than an S.E.C. exam—a broker claims to be a professional. These questions lead to *mutual* understanding. They are even more relevant when you consider that you lose *money* on poor investments while he continues to make commissions. As a customer, don't be bashful!

If on your first meeting, or subsequently, you feel there is little rapport, don't hesitate to go back to the manager. Don't feel embarrassed about telling him you don't care for the broker he has selected. The manager much prefers introducing you to another in his firm to having you take your business to a competitor.

SHOP AROUND

Even though you like the first firm you talk to, don't open an account until you check with another firm or two on your list. One of them may suit you even better and, since interviews take little time, nothing much is lost. The process of opening an account is no more complicated than opening a bank account or retail charge account, so leave this detail to last.

The initial time and effort you spend can be most rewarding. Until you have shopped around you have no idea which firm may be able to help *you* the most, and the wrong selection can cost you money.

When your interviews are completed, review them at home along with any literature you have been given. Just because you have decided to invest, there is no great hurry to put your money in the market. There will be good investments today, tomorrow, next week, next month. Meanwhile your money is secure in the bank.

RESEARCH DEPARTMENTS—ANALYSTS

It is up to your broker to call your attention to investments that his research department recommends for your objectives.

Some firms will also review your portfolio—the collection of stocks and bonds already in your possession—and make recommendations on which stocks should be sold, what others bought. If this service is offered when you are interviewing a broker, accept it. His firm's review will give you an insight into how the firm operates. If you don't already own securities and simply have cash to invest, you may also be offered a possible portfolio. The suggestions are not infallible, but they do provide guidelines. (See also Chapter Ten, "Your Own Investment Ideas.")

When your broker gives you a mass of facts and figures about a company or industry, he is passing on information given him by analysts in his firm's research department. The statistics on *past* performance are *factual;* conclusions about the *future* are *conjecture.* The most you should expect from a research department is an *educated guess* about a company or an industry, not a guarantee.

From time to time, as you read the financial pages of your newspaper, you will see ads from firms offering their latest research on some company or industry. If you're interested in the subject matter, there's no harm in sending a postcard for it. But don't think you will be getting some hot inside information. At best you will become a little more knowledgeable; in return you will have placed your name on a mailing list of prospects for this firm. Like any other free advice, it's cheap, and it will be stale investment information by the time you get it.

Stock analysts are under constant pressure by brokers to come up with good investment suggestions. They usually oblige with quantity, but the quality varies widely. Read as many research reports as you can find time for, but before you tell your broker to buy any of the recommended stocks, *discuss them with him.* He can advise whether or not they are suitable for *your* investment objective, and he will have a pretty good idea of how good the analyst who prepared the report is.

For several years there has been talk of discontinuing publication of free research information in order to reduce brokers' expenses. However, these research reports stimulate trading and also attract new clients, and this results in more commissions. If Procter and Gamble wants to improve profit by selling more soap, they increase advertising and promotion; they don't eliminate them. Free research in one form or another will no doubt be around for quite some time.

OPENING YOUR ACCOUNT

Always remember that brokers are salesmen who are hungry for customers and commissions. This places you in the enviable position of being able to take your time deciding which broker you want to work with. After you have made your decision, opening an account is simple. You give your broker the same type of credit information you would give a department store and also a personal reference or two. Then you are ready to do business. The sample (Figure 2) that follows is typical of forms used by most brokerage firms; it includes all the information required by the S.E.C.

WHEN YOUR BROKER CHANGES FIRMS

Many employees look for another job and when they find it, give their employers two weeks' notice. Thus everyone has a period of transition. Brokers perform differently. They continue business as usual up to the afternoon before they start working for another firm. Right after the market closes for the day they tell the boss their decision and supposedly turn over all their client information. Then they arrange for the immediate transfer of the S.E.C. registration to the new employer so they can start business with him the next day. Of course, your broker has been planning this change for some time and he probably has a duplicate list of clients to take with him.

The first you may know of the change is when you call your broker at the old firm only to find that he is no longer with them and another broker has been assigned to your account. Or perhaps right after the transfer your broker may call to solicit your business for his new firm.

In any event you are faced with the question of staying with your firm or moving with your broker. Your broker will probably suggest that he can provide better service with his new firm. If you have been satisfied with your working relationship with him in the past, by all means move with him and give the new firm a try.

This doesn't mean you have to go through a great formality

NEW ACCOUNT INFORMATION WORKSHEET | DATE

INSTRUCTIONS FOR PREPARING WORKSHEET

INSTRUCTIONS TO R.R.
SUBMIT COMPLETED FORM TO BRANCH OPERATIONS SECTION ON DAY ACCOUNT IS OPENED. ACCOUNT NUMBER WILL BE ASSIGNED ONLY ON RECEIPT OF THIS FORM.

INSTRUCTIONS TO BRANCH OPERATIONS SECTION:
ASSIGN ACCOUNT NUMBER PER S.P.I. PREPARE NEW ACCOUNT INFORMATION CARD
RETAIN THIS WORKSHEET FOR BRANCH RECORDS.

NAME (TITLE, IF ANY – FIRST – MIDDLE – LAST) | BRANCH OFFICE | ACCOUNT NO. | R.R. NUMBER

FED. IDEN. NO. | ☐ SOCIAL SECURITY OR ☐ FEDERAL

ADDRESS (NUMBER & STREET – CITY – ZONE – STATE. IF P.O. BOX, CUSTOMER'S HOME ADDRESS MUST BE ENTERED)

EMPLOYER'S NAME & ADDRESS

NATURE OF BUSINESS | CUSTOMER'S OCCUPATION | HOME TELE. | BUS. TELE.

HUSBAND'S NAME & OCCUPATION | HUSBAND'S EMPLOYER (NAME & NATURE OF BUSINESS)

OVER 21 YRS. OF AGE? ☐ YES ☐ NO | U.S. CITIZEN? ☐ YES ☐ NO | ACCOUNT TYPE ☐ CASH ☐ MARGIN | KIND OF ACCOUNT ☐ STOCK ☐ COMMODITY ☐ STOCK AND COMMODITY | DATE A/C OPENED

NON-RESIDENT ALIEN YES ☐ NO ☐ | WHAT COUNTRY? | FORMER ACCOUNT? ☐ YES ☐ NO IF YES, ENTER PREVIOUS A/C NO. | RELATED TO OFFICER OR EMPLOYEE? ☐ YES ☐ NO IF YES, ENTER NAME & RELATIONSHIP

NAME & ADDRESS OF BANK, BROKER OR COMMERCIAL REFERENCE | HOW LONG HAVE YOU KNOWN CUSTOMER?

REFERENCE CHECKED BY | NAME AND POSITION OF OFFICIAL CONTACTED | IS ADDITIONAL CHECK BY CREDIT DEPT. RECOMMENDED ☐ YES ☐ NO

IF A/C IS ESTATE OR TRUST, ETC. – NAME OF OFFICER | NAME & ADDRESS OF ATTORNEYS/TRUSTEES

LEGAL DOCUMENTS SIGNED
☐ JOINT ACCOUNT AGREEMENT ☐ MARGIN AGREEMENT
☐ POWER OF ATTORNEY ☐ LENDING AGREEMENT
OTHER

SOURCE OF ACCOUNT
☐ ADVERTISING LEAD ☐ LECTURE PROGRAM ☐ CALL IN
☐ DIRECT SOLICITATION BY R.R.
☐ REFERRAL (BY)

SPECIAL MAILING INSTRUCTIONS | SPECIAL-DATA PROCESSING INSTRUCTIONS ☐ DUP. CONFIRM ☐ DUP. STATEMENTS NAME & ADDRESS FOR THESE MAILINGS | AUTOMATIC DIVIDEND ☐ CHECK (✓) THIS BOX IF AUTOMATIC DIVIDEND IS DESIRED.

STANDING INSTRUCTIONS
☐ RECEIVE AND DELIVER (AGAINST FUNDS) ☐ SEND CHECK FOR PROCEEDS OF SALE ☐ SHIP (FREE) ☐ DO NOT TRANSFER AND SHIP SECURITIES

OTHER INSTRUCTIONS:

INITIAL TRANSACTION | R.R.'S SIGNATURE | PRODUCTION UNIT MANAGER'S SIGNATURE

2. New Account Information Work Sheet

of closing your old account—you simply don't give any more orders. In this way, if your new relationship doesn't work out successfully, you can go back to your first firm and interview another broker there.

You may feel at this point that I am placing too much emphasis on interviewing brokers, but consider that the better the understanding between client and broker the better chance there is for a successful relationship. There is enough uncertainty and risk to investing your savings in stocks and bonds without increasing this risk through lack of mutual understanding.

CHAPTER SEVEN

How to Work with Your Broker

HIS RESPONSIBILITY AND YOURS

Now that you have decided on the broker you want to work with, there are ways for you to get the most out of the relationship. Keep in mind that he is *your agent* and acting on your instructions. If your buy and sell orders are not explicit, you stand to be disappointed by his services.

When you go into a store, prices are plainly marked on the merchandise and you either accept or reject them. In contrast, stock transactions are negotiated by the agents of sellers and buyers, and prices may fluctuate rapidly. The type of order you place with your broker may give him more freedom to negotiate a price than you care for him to have. Or it may restrict him to the point where he can't execute your order at all.

MARKET ORDERS

Your broker may quote you a stock price of 30 bid and 30½ asked. This means you can buy a hundred shares at $30.50 per share or sell at $30 because there is at least one firm offer to buy and one firm offer to sell a hundred shares—*one round lot*—at these prices. If the price meets with your approval you give your broker a *market order*—to buy or sell *at the market.* He makes the transaction in your *cash account.* This requires you to pay the full amount of the purchase—or deliver your stock in the case of a sale—within five business days. Saturdays, Sundays, and holidays when the exchanges are closed don't count.

If another investor placed an order ahead of yours and there was only one round lot available at the 30–30½ quote, then the bid and asked prices might change. Your market order would then be executed at the new price that prevailed when your order actually reached the specialist. (See Chapter Eight.) If the stock price is *volatile*, with large rapid changes, you may find your market order was executed at a price higher or lower than you had expected or had been quoted.

LIMIT ORDERS

You can avoid this unexpected and sometimes embarrassing situation by restricting your broker to an exact price, but this has a disadvantage: it prevents him from *negotiating* the price of the transaction. The compromise is the *limit order*. It's like asking a friend to buy something for you at an auction. You tell her how much you want to pay but you give some leeway to pay a little more if necessary, though not an unlimited amount.

In the same way, you tell your broker to buy the stock at the quoted $30.50 price with a quarter point—one point is $1.00—discretion. He can now go up to $30.75 *if necessary*, but he is supposed to buy it at the best possible price.

The limit order may also be used when selling. If the quoted bid price for your stock is $30 you can tell your broker that you will sell at this price but give him the discretion to accept a little less if necessary to make the trade.

The amount of discretion you permit depends first on how much money you have to invest or on the minimum you will accept for your stock. The price of the stock also influences the amount of discretion. A quarter of a point discretion for a $30 stock may be adequate, while three points—$3.00—may be necessary for a high-priced stock like IBM. From a percentage standpoint, both would be about the same. A third factor is the volatility of the stock's price. The greater and faster the price tends to change the greater the discretion should be. *Always be specific about how much discretion or variance from the quoted price you are allowing your broker.*

The limit order avoids misunderstandings with your broker by establishing guidelines within which he can work to best advantage for you.

TRADING ON MARGIN

The average small investor may deprive herself of a valuable investment procedure on the mistaken grounds that trading on margin is too risky and too complicated. It's not that complicated, but first you must understand the risk type of margin trading in order to appreciate the *conservative* use of margin.

A *margin account* differs from your cash account in that at least part of your stock transaction is done with money or securities *borrowed from your broker*, and you must keep some cash or securities on deposit with him as collateral. The Federal Reserve Board specifies the maximum amount that may be borrowed, and your broker will charge you interest on what he lends just as your bank would. At one time the margin requirement may be 90 per cent and you can borrow only 10 per cent of the total amount of the transaction. Another time it may be 60 per cent and you can borrow 40 per cent. In times of recession the Federal Reserve will lower margin requirements. This permits you to borrow more. In times of inflation the margin will be raised and you may borrow less. Margin limits are simply one tool at the disposal of the Federal Reserve to keep the national economy on an even keel.

Occasionally the Exchange may stipulate a 100 per cent margin requirement for a particular stock if it is considered that there is undue speculation and trading. The 100 per cent margin eliminates all those who borrow money to buy the stock, and the reduced demand for the stock slows the price spiral.

BUYING ON MARGIN—RISKY

In 1970 you could have invested $10,000 in Dr. Pepper, buying 1,000 shares. By the end of 1972 your investment would have been worth $26,000, a gain of 160 per cent. Had the stock been bought on margin in 1970, you would have needed only $6,500 cash to buy 1,000 shares—borrowing $3,500 from your broker. When you sold the stock at the end of 1972 for $26,000 and repaid your broker his $3,500, you would have made $22,500. This is equal to a gain of 330 per cent on your $6,500, even after you paid $1,000 or so interest on your loan.

This is a type of *leverage*—using someone else's money to increase your profit potential—that can be very risky. Had the price of the stock dropped substantially you would have lost much of your $6,500, and you would still owe your broker $3,500 plus interest.

SELLING SHORT—RISKY MARGIN TRADING

Just as you can borrow money from your broker, you can also borrow stock and sell it; this is called *selling short*. In 1970, had you decided that the value of Grumman Corporation stock would decline, you could have *borrowed one hundred shares and sold them* for $2,200. By the end of 1972 you could have repaid the hundred borrowed shares by buying the stock for $1,000. The profit on the short sale would have been $1,200—the difference between what you sold the borrowed stock for and what you had to pay for the stock to repay the broker.

The risk, of course, was that the stock might have gone up in price, and it would have cost you more to repay the borrowed stock than the $2,200 you received when you sold. As with buying on margin, you are required to have collateral for the value of the borrowed stock. Selling short is best left to the investor who can afford considerable risk.

THE UP-TICK

If the price of a stock is falling, speculators will want to sell it short so as to make a profit on the declining price. If this speculative selling were extensive it would cause the price to drop still further and faster. Then, when the speculators started to "cover" their short sales—buy back to repay the borrowed stock—the price would start to rise abnormally fast. To reduce the possibility of wild price fluctuations, an "up-tick" is required before a stock can be sold short. An up-tick is simply the sale of a stock at *any price higher than its preceding sale price.*

The price of a series of trades in a stock you want to sell short may look like this: 45, 44¼, 44, 43½, 43, 42½, 42, 41, 41¼, 41. The short sale could not be made until a trade had been made at 41¼. At that price the sale was higher then the preceding sale—an up-tick of a quarter point—and your short sale order could be executed. At that point the price of the stock would have already dropped 8 per cent. If you wanted to sell short at 45 in anticipation of a 10 per cent drop, the sale would no longer be worth while and you would cancel the order. The requirement for an up-tick, therefore, reduces selling pressure.

CONSERVATIVE TRADING ON MARGIN

Since conservative investors don't want to incur the risks of buying on margin or selling short, they all too often close their minds to anything that even sounds like it. Selling "short against the box" has this high-risk *implication*, but in actuality it is ultra-conservative. It is a means whereby you can *protect a profit and defer capital gains taxes* on a stock *you already own.* Instead of borrowing stock from your broker to sell short in anticipation of the price dropping, you "borrow" the stock *from your safety deposit box.* You give this stock to your broker as collateral and then sell the stock short. It works this way:

In July 1966, I bought two hundred shares of Freeport Sulphur —now called Freeport Minerals—for $8,932.26. Fifteen months later—October 1967—the investment was worth $14,247.35 for a *paper profit* of $5,000. The wise move was to turn my profit on paper into a cash profit by selling the stock, but my taxes for the year were already high. By selling short against the box the *profit was assured* but the *taxes were deferred.* Here is what took place:

When the order was placed with the broker he lent me two hundred shares of Freeport and sold them. At the same time I took *my* two hundred shares from my safety deposit box and sent them to him as collateral. The proceeds from the sale of the borrowed stock were credited to my account and available for buying other securities. In January 1968—the following tax year—I repaid the borrowed stock by transferring ownership of my shares to the broker and realized a taxable gain. It made no difference whether the price of the stock soared or dropped out of sight after I made the sale short against the box—I had my $5,000 profit and the broker was holding the two hundred shares of Freeport that I owed him.

There is another situation where selling short against the box can be profitable for the conservative investor. If you suspect a drop in the price of a stock which you have owned for a long time and which has appreciated tremendously, you can protect your paper profit with a *minimum of immediate tax consequence.* As an example, a $1,500 investment in Philip Morris in 1966 would be worth $13,000 in early 1973. If you foresaw a serious price decline but felt it would recover to become a good long-term investment several months later, you could *protect* your profit and *delay* the full tax by selling short in this way.

When you sell short against the box for $13,000, no tax is due *at that time* on the gain. A few months later the stock could have been bought back for $11,000–15 per cent less–to repay the borrowed stock. You would have had a taxable gain of $2,000 –the difference between your selling and repurchase price– and you would continue to own your stock for a good long-term investment.

Had the price not declined as you anticipated but gone up, you could always have delivered your stock to "cover" your short position–pay off the borrowed value. You would then have had to be satisfied with the gain from $1,500 to $13,000. You would pay the full capital gains tax, and you would no longer own the stock as a long-term investment.

Understand that selling short against the box does not *avoid* capital gains tax but simply *delays* it while you *protect your profit.* Selling short is highly risky, but selling short against the box is very conservative and a valuable investment procedure.

STOP ORDERS

Possibly you have heard of stop loss orders. They are in fact simply *stop orders;* they *minimize* your loss but by no means stop it. You may buy a $50 stock with the idea that it will go up in value, but you may not be willing to lose more than 10 per cent–$5.00 per share–in case it goes down. To protect yourself, you can place a stop sell order at $45 at the time you buy at $50. If the stock goes up, nothing happens to your stop sell order and your investment increases in value.

If the price drops and the stock is traded at $45, your stop sell order is automatically changed into a market order to sell. Your stock is then sold for whatever price is then bid. This is not necessarily your stop price of $45 but is as close to it as your broker can negotiate. In the case of a rapidly falling stock, there may be a great many market orders ahead of yours. Then your actual sale price might be considerably less than your stop price.

The reverse of the stop sell order is the stop buy order. This may be used as protection for short and short-against-the-box sales. If you have sold borrowed stock at $45, expecting the price to decline to $40, and it rises instead, you want to minimize your loss when you have to buy stock to repay the loan. A stop buy order at $50 would automatically become a market order if the price went up to $50 instead of down as you had hoped.

A conservative investor can also use the stop buy order to advantage. You may watch the price of a stock decline slowly week after week and decide that when it gets down to a certain point you will buy it. Let's say the price drops gradually from 26 to 23—about 10 per cent. At that price it looks like a good buy. Unfortunately it still doesn't give any indication of starting to rise again, so you are hesitant about buying now if you can buy it for less later. Rather than risk a sudden change, you can place a stop buy order at 23. In another few days, if you can buy it for less, so much the better, but if it suddenly goes up your stop buy order is changed automatically to a market order and your broker buys the stock for you. You will not have missed a good investing opportunity.

OPEN ORDERS

At the time you give your broker an order you can specify its duration. You can give a *day order*, which must be executed on the day you give it or it is automatically canceled. You can also give an order which is *good until a specific date*, after which the order is automatically canceled. Or you can give an order *good until canceled* by you, which is an *open order*. If you tell your broker to sell at a certain price and he is unable to do so immediately, you should tell him to cancel the order. Otherwise you may find a month or two later, when it is no longer advisable to sell, that the order has finally been carried out.

The same applies to buying a stock—you may find that you have already invested your money elsewhere when your buy order is finally executed. Your broker is supposed to keep you posted on your open orders as a customer service, but he is not legally required to do so. The responsibility is yours and, to prevent embarrassment, you are better off canceling any orders your broker cannot execute on your terms. See sample (Figure 3) of open order confirmation that follows.

WORKING WITH YOUR BROKER

Misunderstanding is the greatest cause of dissension between customer and broker. Now that you know the types of orders available to you, give him *specific* buy and sell instructions. Don't tell him to buy at a quoted asking price of 17 if you really meant at 17 with discretion to go a quarter or half point higher if necessary. By the same token don't tell him to buy at the market if you really meant a maximum price—the stock may have moved to 18½ after he quoted 17. As your agent, he is supposed to carry out your *instructions as you gave them* and not as you were *thinking* about giving them. Your broker doesn't have second sight. His confirmation of your order will show exactly how the order was entered, and you should check it carefully to make sure any misunderstanding is caught immediately. (See samples of confirmation and monthly statement, Figures 4 and 5.)

Between the mid-1940s and mid-1960s most investors were pleased with their brokers' recommendations. The Standard & Poor's Index of 425 Industrial Stocks rose from 15 to 100—almost 700 per cent—and virtually every recommended stock showed improvement. From the late 1960s to 1974 this index has ranged from 100 down to 70, back up to 120, and back down again, and successful recommendations were much harder, almost impossible, to make. Brokers bore the blame. The point to remember is that nobody forced you to follow your broker's advice on how to invest *your money*, and he offered it in good faith simply as a service. (See Chapter Nine, "Outside Advice and Assistance.")

White, Weld & Co.
Incorporated

OFFICE AT New York One Liberty Plaza
DATE November 15, 1974
ACCOUNT NO. 20-7801-05-114

WE CONFIRM THAT WE HAVE Entered OPEN ORDER(S) FOR YOUR ACCOUNT: PLEASE CHECK THE FOLLOWING ITEM(S) WITH YOUR RECORDS AND ADVISE US IMMEDIATELY IF THERE ARE ANY DISCREPANCIES.

TO BUY	TO SELL
100 Shares General Motors Corporation @32 1/4 GTC (Good Till Canceled)	

Miss Nicole C. Verbal
5758 No. South Street
Anytown, New York 10009

IMPORTANT—PLEASE READ CAREFULLY

AS THE RESPONSIBILITY FOR FAILURE TO CANCEL AN EXISTING ORDER WHEN ENTERING A SUBSTITUTE ORDER THEREFORE RESTS UPON THE CUSTOMER, TRANSACTIONS RESULTING FROM THE EXECUTION OF ANY OR BOTH SUCH ORDERS WILL BE ENTERED IN THE CUSTOMER'S ACCOUNT.

WHEN A SECURITY IS EX-DIVIDEND, EX-INTEREST, EX-RIGHTS OR EX-DISTRIBUTION, THE FOLLOWING TYPE OF OPEN ORDERS WILL BE REDUCED BY THE VALUE OF SUCH PAYMENT, RIGHTS OR DISTRIBUTION UNLESS OTHERWISE SPECIFIED.

1. BUY 2. SELL STOP 3. SELL STOP LIMIT

THE FOLLOWING TYPE OF OPEN ORDERS ARE UNAFFECTED.

1. SELL 2. BUY STOP 3. BUY STOP LIMIT

3. Open Order Confirmation

There's no exact standard for what is too much trading—*churning*—or too little, but don't forget your broker is working for commissions. It is only natural for him to want you to trade frequently. If he suggests that you sell a stock that he recommended you buy only a few weeks or months earlier, insist that he give you good reasons. Just as you watch to see if a stock goes up when he recommends it, you should watch to see if a stock goes down after he has suggested you sell it. This will give an indication of whether it was a valid suggestion or if it merely made another commission.

Dividends can also be a cause for misunderstanding between you and your broker. The board of directors of a company declares the dividend. They decide it will be paid on a certain date—*payment date*—but to make sure that all checks are made out properly and in the mail on time, a *record date* is specified, possibly a month earlier. Every stockholder on record as of the record date is eligible to receive the dividend on the payment date.

The misunderstanding develops because people think that if they buy the stock on the record date they will receive the dividend. It's obvious that *if you buy on the record date, the company's records of stockholders won't include your name and you won't get the dividend.* You must own the stock five business days before the record date, which is the *ex-dividend* date. In this way time is allowed for you to pay for the stock and the company to change records of ownership.

Significant dates may be like this: November 10, ex-dividend; November 16—five business days later—record date; and December 9, payment date. Too often investors are disgruntled because they do not understand the difference between ex-dividend and record dates.

You can appreciate the fact that if you are a small investor—either in dollars or in number of trades—your commissions don't permit your broker to spend as much time with you as with a large investor. If he seems to be ignoring you, possibly he feels your investments are achieving your objectives and there is no need to bother you. Don't let this stop you from calling him whenever you have a question. He is there to serve you. He will

4. Order Confirmation

TRADE DATE MO.	DAY	YR.	SETTLEMENT DATE MO.	DAY	YR.
02	24	75	03	03	75

DATE DUE

White, Weld & Co.
Incorporated

WE DESIRE TO CONFIRM THE FOLLOWING TRANSACTION FOR YOUR ACCOUNT, SUBJECT TO THE AGREEMENT AND CONDITIONS PRINTED ON THE REVERSE SIDE.

CODES *	MKT. *	INT USE

*SEE REVERSE SIDE HEREOF FOR CAPACITY IN WHICH WE ACTED, MARKET AND EXPLANATION OF CODES.

(BOT) = YOU BOUGHT (SLD) = YOU SOLD — SECURITY DESCRIPTION

BOT 100 Delta Air Lines, Inc.

PRICE: 30 3/4

AMOUNT	INTEREST/DIVIDEND	STATE TAX	COMMISSION	S.E.C. FEE	MISC.
3075.00			57.38		

OFF.	ACCOUNT NO.	T	PROD.	BILLING DATE
20	7801	5	114	2/24/75

TYPE OF ACCT. 0. MARGIN 1. SHORT 2. SPECIAL BOND 4. SUBSCRIPTION 5. CASH 6. MISC.

NET AMOUNT: $3,132.38

Miss Nicole C. Verbal
5758 North South Street
Anytown, N. Y. 10009

White, Weld & Co.
Incorporated

1 American Row
Hartford, Conn.
06103

PLEASE ENCLOSE THIS STUB WITH ALL PAYMENTS AND SECURITIES TO THE ADDRESS SHOWN ABOVE.

OFF.	ACCOUNT NO.	T	PROD.
20	7801	5	114

SEC. NO.	TRANS NO.
20450	736284

INTERNAL USE

THIS CONFIRMATION SHALL BE DEEMED CORRECT IN ALL RESPECTS UNLESS WRITTEN NOTICE OF ANY INACCURACY IS SENT FORTHWITH TO US.
On other than round lots (normally 100 shares) on all exchanges an amount has been added to the price on purchases or deducted on sales. On the New York Stock Exchange this amount is 12½¢ per share In all other cases an explanation will be provided on request

NEW YORK • BOSTON • CHICAGO • ATLANTA
DALLAS • HARTFORD • HOUSTON • LOS ANGELES
MINNEAPOLIS • NEW HAVEN • PHILADELPHIA • SAN FRANCISCO
LONDON • PARIS • ZURICH • CARACAS
GENEVA • HONG KONG • MONTREAL

ACCOUNT NUMBER	PERIOD ENDING	PAGE
20 07801 05 114	03/29/74	1

Miss Nicole C. Verbal
5758 North South Street
Anytown, N. Y. 10009

DATE MO. DAY	BOUGHT OR RECEIVED	SOLD OR DELIVERED
02 05	5,000.00	
02 07	100	
02 07	100	
02 07		5,000.00
02 10		
02 24		100
02 24		100
02 27	300	

IF THIS IS A "MARGIN" ACCOUNT, IT IS A COMBINED STATEMENT OF YOUR GENERAL ACCOUNT AND OF A SPECIAL MISCELLANEOUS ACCOUNT MAINTAINED FOR YOU UNDER SECTION 4 (F) (6) OF REGULATION T ISSUED BY THE BOARD OF GOVERNORS OF THE FEDERAL RESERVE SYSTEM. THE PERMANENT RECORD OF THE SEPARATE ACCOUNT AS REQUIRED BY REGULATION T IS AVAILABLE FOR INSPECTION UPON REQUEST.

IMPORTANT

YOU ARE REFERRED TO THE ADVICES PREVIOUSLY SENT YOU CONCERNING THE TRANSACTIONS LISTED HEREON, WHICH INDICATE WHETHER WE ACTED IN CONNECTION WITH SUCH TRANSACTIONS AS AGENTS, OR AS PRINCIPALS FOR OUR ACCOUNT.
A FINANCIAL STATEMENT OF THIS FIRM IS AVAILABLE FOR YOUR PERSONAL INSPECTION AT ITS OFFICES, OR A COPY OF IT WILL BE MAILED UPON YOUR WRITTEN REQUEST.

CORRECTIONS

THIS STATEMENT SHALL BE DEEMED CORRECT IN ALL RESPECTS UNLESS WRITTEN NOTICE OF ANY INACCURACY IS SENT FORTHWITH TO US.

INTEREST CALCULATION

INTEREST, IF ANY, IS CALCULATED FOR THE PERIOD COVERED BY THIS STATEMENT, IN THE MANNER DESCRIBED IN OUR "INTEREST STATEMENT." THIS INTEREST CHARGE WILL APPEAR ON YOUR NEXT STATEMENT.

PRESERVE THIS STATEMENT

PLEASE PRESERVE THIS STATEMENT. YOU WILL REQUIRE THE INFORMATION THEREON FOR THE PREPARATION OF YOUR INCOME TAX RETURN AND TO VERIFY INTEREST CHARGES APPEARING ON SUBSEQUENT STATEMENTS.

SEE REVERSE SIDE FOR AGREEMENT

5. Monthly Statement

appreciate it and have more time to give you if you call after the market closes.

ABOUT COMMISSIONS

I will not dwell on brokers' commissions because extensive arguments on the subject have been presented to the S.E.C. and commissions are still in a state of flux.

Furthermore, a great deal of the hue and cry about large brokers' commissions is brought on by the fact that the dollar amount must be shown on your confirmation. Expressed in dollars, it appears large, but as a percentage of the total transaction it is not. I recently bought Eastman Kodak stock for a client and the commission was a whopping $448.50 and yet it represented less than one per cent of the total cost of $58,273.50. Had I

White, Weld & Co.
Incorporated
55 WATER STREET, NEW YORK, N. Y. 10041

MEMBERS OF THE FOLLOWING STOCK EXCHANGES
NEW YORK • AMERICAN • MIDWEST
PACIFIC COAST • BOSTON

1

DESCRIPTION	PRICE	CHARGE OR PURCHASES	CREDIT OR SALES	ACCT TYPE	ACCOUNT NUMBER / COMMISSION
CASH ACCOUNT				5	
NTS.CITICORP 9.70% FLOATING RATE JD JUNE 1989 /REGD./	RECD			5	
DELTA AIR LINES INC.	30 3/4	3,132.38		5	
NORTHWEST AIRLINES	15 7/8	1,625.19		5	
NTS.CITICORP 9.70% FLOATING RATE JD JUNE 1989 /REGD./	99 3/8		5,027.57	5	
		270.00		5	
CHECK PAID					
BAL DUE					
DELTA AIR LINES INC.	SHIP			5	
NORTHWEST AIRLINES	SHIP			5	
TRAVELERS CORP.	RECD			5	
CLOSING BALANCE			00		

REGISTERED REPRESENTATIVE

ACCOUNT TYPE
0. MARGIN
1. SHORT
2. SPECIAL BOND
3. SPEC. CONV. DEBT SECUR.
4. SUBSCRIPTION
5. CASH
6. MISC.
7. SPECIAL MISC.
8. INCOME
9. SECURITY LOANED

bought a house for the same amount, the real estate agent would have received about $3,500, and a jeweler's profit on a diamond of the same value would have been four times that amount. This, of course, is a huge investment, but I also recently bought a hundred shares of stock at 4¼ on which the commission was $16.39 or 3.7 per cent, which more nearly resembles the supermarket's profit.

It is my belief that commissions have to be looked upon simply as a cost of doing business. Whether that cost is high or low, you are paying for three basic services: stock traded at the most advantageous price to you; money from a sale credited to your account or sent to you promptly and without question; new certificates sent promptly. Any extra services that the broker offers are simply to meet the competition of other brokerage firms.

CHAPTER EIGHT

Stock Exchanges

THE WAY THEY OPERATE

You will buy and sell your securities through your broker. Most books written by members of the broker community dwell in great detail on the workings of the various exchanges. After all, this is where *they* transact your business. I don't believe you need to know the finite details of the exchanges in order to invest, any more than you need to know how to assemble a car just to drive.

The important point to understand is how your broker finds a buyer or seller for you *when you want to trade.* It also helps to understand the advantages and disadvantages of having your stocks traded Over-the-Counter, on the American Exchange, on the New York Stock Exchange, or on some other market. Perhaps it will be easiest if we follow the development of the Pseudo Corporation, which we formed in Chapter One.

OVER-THE-COUNTER MARKET

When the Pseudo Corporation offers its stock for sale to outsiders—"goes public"—some provision must be made for subsequent stock trading. A broker familiar with the company may *make a market* in the stock by finding either buyers or sellers of the stock. Initially, he may trade for his own account. This means he will buy stock being offered for sale and hold it until such time as he can find another buyer. When a buyer does come along the broker can sell the stock he owns or he can find another investor who may be willing to sell. This is trading *over the counter* in its simplest form.

If you want to sell Pseudo stock, which you feel is worth $10, you *offer* it with $10 as the *asking price*. A buyer may consider it worth only $9.00; so that is what he *bids* for it. If you and the buyer are adamant, no trade takes place. When another investor expresses interest, the broker can quote a *bid price* of $9.00 and an *asking price* of $10. The broker takes the part of an arbitrator; he may get both sides to settle for $9.50. This then becomes the *last trade price*.

As the Pseudo Corporation's reputation grows and the broker becomes more active in trading it, he may buy and sell for his own account or he may arrange trades between two investors, or between an investor and another broker, or between two brokers for their clients. In this way trades are expedited and there is a continuing supply and demand. Several brokers may eventually make a market in Pseudo stock, quoting Over-the-Counter bid and asked prices and having a readily available number of investors.

The National Association of Securities Dealers (N.A.S.D.) provides members with a current list of brokers who make a market in Over-the-Counter securities. Brokers from all over the country can thus get an immediate quotation on Pseudo or other Over-the-Counter stocks. The most actively traded are quoted daily in the financial pages of the larger newspapers.

It is apparent that when a company's stock is traded over the counter there is no reason for you to believe or assume that the company is financially sound. The quality of stocks ranges from those of struggling new companies with minimum financing and experience to old, well-established firms. Indeed, the stock of Chase Manhattan Bank until 1965 was only traded over the counter.

The moral is, *when you buy Over-the-Counter, be sure to investigate a company's finances and capabilities very carefully.*

EXCHANGE LISTING

Both the American and New York Stock exchanges have minimum requirements for a stock that is *listed and traded* on the exchange floor. These include such things as minimum number of shares available for trading, number of stockholders, years of profitable operation, and so forth. The requirements are more stringent for the New York Exchange than for the American but, for both, the purpose is to create the largest possible market for quality stocks.

Usually a company first applies for listing on the American Exchange and then after meeting stricter requirements it may apply for listing on the New York Exchange. If a company's stock is listed on one exchange and then is transferred to the other it is automatically dropped—*delisted*—from the first exchange. Because of the listing requirements, there is less investigating for you to do before you invest in a listed stock.

BENEFITS OF EXCHANGE LISTING

Both you and the company benefit when a stock is listed on one of the national exchanges. Because your stock is traded in one central location, everyone interested in buying or selling must of necessity converge at that point. Your stock, therefore, gets the greatest exposure to investors from all over the country. You have an improved chance of either selling or buying at a moment's notice.

Past experience shows that exchange listing does not avoid stock price manipulation or corporate shenanigans. Management of Equity Funding, listed on the New York Stock Exchange in 1973, was accused of writing fictitious insurance policies and juggling the accounts to make the company look far more prosperous than it actually was. The glare of publicity associated with an exchange listing, however, reduces these possibilities and the frequency with which they might otherwise occur.

This same publicity simplifies the company's job if it becomes necessary to sell more stocks or bonds, because the company is already well known among investors. As soon as the Pseudo Corporation could meet the listing requirements, it would be advantageous to have the stock traded on a large exchange rather than Over-the-Counter.

TRADING PROCEDURE

When you place an order with your broker to buy or sell he calls his representative on the floor of the exchange where the stock is traded. Your order is taken to a certain location—

post—where the stock of this particular company is traded. Other brokers with buy and sell orders also meet there and continuous trading goes on.

Obviously, if many sellers and buyers of a particular stock are congregated at the post, there must be some method for them to identify one another in order to make a trade. The exchange assigns a *specialist* to perform this function for specific stocks. He quotes the price one broker is willing to pay for the stock and the price another broker is willing to sell the stock for. If they are reasonably close, he identifies one to the other and they conclude the trade, reporting back the price to the specialist. The specialist can then quote bid and asked prices as well as the price of the last trade.

If the price difference between the offer to buy and the offer to sell is too great, then the specialist is expected to use his own money to buy or his own stock to sell in order to close the gap. The specialist is expected to maintain an *orderly market* —buying stock when there are too many sellers and selling stock when there are too many buyers. He does this with his own finances—not the exchange's—and therefore must have an inventory of stock. The objective is to minimize large fluctuations between trade prices. On a larger scale he functions much the same as the broker who makes a market in Pseudo Corporation stock.

As soon as your broker's representative on the floor of the exchange negotiates your order, results are relayed to your broker. He then calls you with the results. The process may take only fifteen minutes anywhere in the country.

Neither the brokers on the floor of the exchange nor the specialists are employees of the exchange. They must pay for membership, which entitles them to transact business there; the commissions you pay provide their income. The specialist further risks making large gains and also large losses when he is required to buy and sell stock with his own finances.

There is presently a great deal of research going on with the aim of merging all stock trading and having it handled by a giant computer. Just one of the many problems to be resolved is that of maintaining an orderly market. Regardless of what changes may come about, the objective is to bring together the greatest number of buyers and sellers of any one particular stock. In this way you, the investor, could be provided with the best potential to buy or sell stocks at fair prices.

CHAPTER NINE

Outside Advice and Assistance

BROKERS, BANKS, PERSONAL ADVISERS

Regardless of the size of your portfolio—$5,000, $100,000, or more—you can benefit from good advice. The advice you want is not only which securities to buy and when but, equally important, *when to sell* and *when to put your money in the bank* instead of into stocks and bonds. Too often a well-meaning friend will suggest a stock that is "bound to go up." You buy it and it does well for a time, but your friend forgets to tell you when to sell. This lack of follow-through can cost you not only a temporary paper profit but possibly a good part of your original investment. It can also hurt you if you invest for income and the suggested stock stops paying dividends.

Underlying this entire topic of getting advice is the fact that it is your money. You must supplement the advice with as much investment knowledge as possible. Brokerage firms often hold seminars to explain investing to potential clients. Your school district may have an adult education course on investing. Why not attend one of these? A lot of what you hear may be old hat to you, but something new and helpful may come up. You can also expand your knowledge by questioning the speaker. A word of caution, though. Don't invest fast in any stock recommended at such a lecture. Take time to investigate. The son of one of my clients invested in such a stock and it rose from 16 to 23 after the course was over. The lecturer wasn't around to tell him when to sell, so he watched the recommended stock slide down to 5⅛.

Investment advice is no different from health, legal, or tax advice. There is plenty of it around for free, but for professional and personalized advice you have to pay.

WHERE TO GET RELIABLE ADVICE

Three general areas of advice are available to you: *your broker* in conjunction with his firm's research department; *subscription investment letters;* and *paid portfolio managers.* They have one feature in common: they do not have a crystal ball that guarantees you will make money. If they did, you can be sure they would become millionaires before they started telling you how to handle your money.

What they can do is evaluate the economic and political factors that influence stock prices and also give you a dispassionate appraisal of your securities. Too many portfolios include "sacred stocks"—inherited perhaps or held long past their peak performance. It might be difficult for you to weed out these stocks, but the outside adviser has no such emotional ties and would be quick to sell them.

Perhaps their third advantage is that they offer someone other than yourself to take the blame when investments don't work out—you can always fire your adviser.

YOUR BROKER AS ADVISER

The least expensive source of advice is your broker's research department. Your trading commissions pay the cost of research if you trade often enough. Unfortunately the recent diminished trading by small investors has reduced brokers' profits, and this free advice may soon come to an end. In the meantime a reliable broker's advice can be a big help if you are a small investor and not interested in paying a third party.

If you depend on a broker, be prepared to keep a closer watch on stocks you buy, hold, or sell than you would if you were paying separately for the advice. Your broker has many clients and if you don't trade actively he may overlook the fact that you own XYZ stock when his analyst recommends it be sold. Ask him periodically, once a month or so, for his opinion on the stocks he has recommended. Ask him also what particular effect his recommendation will have on your total portfolio.

But *don't confuse investment advice with portfolio supervision.*

The two common complaints about brokers are that they try to make commissions on too much buying and selling and that they recommend stocks because their firms act as underwriters. (See Chapter Fifteen, "New Issues and Secondary Offerings.") These complaints may sometimes be valid, but if you have selected your broker carefully and you yourself follow your investments carefully, you should be able to profit from your broker's advice.

When the market and the economy are in a slump the advice least often given by a broker and least often followed by investors is to sell stocks, take profits or losses, and put your money in the bank. Too often the tendency is to switch from one losing stock to another in the futile hope of finding a winner. Successful millionaire investors like Jesse Livermore and Bernard Baruch were famous for their practice of selling and staying on the sidelines until the situation turned around. If *all* your money is not invested all the time, don't worry; you are using good investment strategy.

INVESTMENT ADVICE BY MAIL

Subscription advisory services have helped a lot of investors. You see ads for them in most financial publications; subscription rates and frequency of publication vary widely. "Moody's Stock Survey" and "The Value Line Investment Survey" are among the many that have been around for quite a time. Some services offer cut-rate trial subscriptions. These give you an excellent opportunity to study their current recommendations. You can watch those stocks—*without investing*—to judge their performance. You shouldn't buy any of these recommendations because your trial subscription will no doubt run out before you are told when to sell.

Ordinarily subscription services list *selected stocks* for different objectives. From time to time they give recommendations to buy or sell as circumstances warrant. By the end of your trial subscription you will have some idea of how good the recommendations have been and whether or not you want to subscribe. Some publications also offer a review of your portfolio and give specific recommendations to whet your interest in subscribing.

If you decide to follow the advice of a subscription service, follow the *current* recommendations to buy. Don't buy a stock recommended a month or two earlier that has done so well that the very next issue recommends selling it for a profit. If you decide to follow the advice, give your broker the order at once. And if you subscribe to several services, *act on the recommendations of only one* so that you can judge where the credit or blame lies for your *total portfolio performance.*

YOUR OWN PAID ADVISER

A third source of advice is the paid portfolio manager who supervises *your* investments on a continuing basis. Busy businesswomen, retired persons, widows who want to be free to travel, women who suddenly inherit money or securities and have little knowledge of investing find this individual service invaluable. The fee is usually a *small* percentage of the market value of your portfolio computed at the time you engage the manager. It will be adjusted quarterly or semi-annually depending on your schedule of payments for the service. The fee is not based on the number of transactions as with a broker; nor does it matter whether your investments are in stocks, bonds, or kept as cash in savings accounts. You are hiring a specialist —like your lawyer or accountant—to work *for you.*

Some brokerage firms offer this service apart from their regular business and charge a separate fee for it. You might assume that this special department gets inside information from the underwriting department. As a matter of fact the S.E.C. requires that the portfolio advisory service be kept separate from the underwriting so that portfolio managers won't help sell a questionable new issue or secondary offering.

I question the concept that this right hand is not supposed to know what that left hand is doing. It defies the precept that top management should oversee *all* departments for the success of the whole. Possibly I am overly suspicious, but personally I would never depend on investment advice from a department so closely related to a brokerage firm, even if the service operated under a different name, as sometimes happens.

Trust departments of most commercial banks also provide portfolio management for their clients. It is a part of their normal business of managing trust funds, estates, and retirement funds. For the sake of efficiency, they usually require *discretionary power* over your portfolio; they not only make decisions but buy, sell, and hold your securities for safekeeping. As with the brokerage advisory service, the trust department is supposed to operate as a separate entity. Their recommendations are not supposed to be influenced by large corporate borrowers or depositors.

For small portfolios, the bank may request your approval to "co-mingle" your account, that is, to combine your account with others that have the same objectives. This arrangement turns out to be rather like a mutual fund. The bank gives you the advantage of diversification, professional management, and lower broker commissions, but you retain a degree of management. If you turn over your portfolio to a trust department for management, be specific about your objectives and be sure the trust officer fully understands. For a reasonable fee the trust department will relieve you of *all* the work. It will give you a summary of your portfolio periodically, complete with amounts of income, capital gains, and losses. This is a great convenience, for it is the only record you need keep for tax purposes.

Some trust departments also offer an automatic investing or reinvesting service. Under the automatic plan, you give them a specific amount of money on a regular schedule, say, monthly; they invest this in a stock of *your choice*. In the reinvestment plan, dividends paid on your stock are reinvested in more stock of the same company. These plans vary somewhat from one bank to another, but both are excellent methods for accumulating more shares of stock with small commissions. And they establish a regular savings plan for you, good if you find it hard to save on your own. But keep in mind that the stock you buy is of your choice, and not necessarily recommended by the bank.

THE INDEPENDENT ADVISER

If you want to participate more actively in managing your portfolio than the trust department permits or want to be further removed from your broker's firm, think about an independent investment adviser.

This specialist is *paid by you* to give investment advice *for your benefit.* Because he is independent, terms of service vary widely. Some specialists simply furnish you with portfolio advice and you make the actual trades; others require full discretion. Some require a minimum portfolio of six figures; others accept a portfolio worth $5,000 or $10,000. Fees also vary but are usually pegged to the total value of your portfolio. Usually the larger the portfolio the greater the fee in dollars, but it is then a smaller percentage of the total. Your participation in management, therefore, depends on the particular service you select and are willing to pay for.

Don't think that this specialized service is only available to wealthy investors. Your accountant, lawyer, or broker either knows or can find an adviser suitable for you. Discuss advisers also with your friends who may have objectives similar to yours and are in comparable tax brackets. You may discover that a personal adviser has been handling their investments successfully for years. But don't just accept the first adviser, talk to several. Settle on one who gives you confidence and with whom you can work comfortably.

ARE ADVISERS RELIABLE?

If you mean can you rely on them to make your portfolio grow in value under all conditions, the answer would have to be "no." In a deteriorating market they have no superhuman powers to insure gains, but they should be able to hold losses lower than you could on your own. In a rising market they should help you achieve your objective and make money for you.

If by "reliable" you mean honest, then the answer is "yes." Any advisory service that manages discretionary portfolios—that is, *has control* over your securities and cash—is required by the S.E.C. to submit to an annual *surprise audit* by an outside auditor. At that time a report is made to the S.E.C. as to whether clients' funds and securities are all accounted for. Even if advisers don't handle discretionary accounts, they operate under the watchful eye of the S.E.C.; in some states there is a commission that supervises activities to guard against fraud.

You should select a personal investment adviser with the same care you use in selecting a broker. (See Chapter Six, "How to Select a Broker.") When a possible new client comes to me, if he or she doesn't ask me all the questions I feel should be asked, I make it a point of giving what I consider essential information about my years of experience, my training, and the types of clients I advise—businesswomen, widows, retired couples, divorcees, housewives usually with their husbands, and various others. If I've made boners as I did in 1973 when I recommended several stocks that lost 20 per cent or so, I tell them about it; I also let them hear about certain stocks that have advanced more than 20 per cent in which I've made considerable money for clients. And I mention municipal and "flower" bonds that have been a comfort to those in the higher tax brackets.

As with brokers and exchanges, you are free to go to the S.E.C. or to the state commission if you have reason to believe there has been skulduggery. The matter will be investigated and remedial action taken if appropriate. But don't complain to the S.E.C. when your adviser's recommendation does not fare as well as you anticipated.

WORKING WITH YOUR ADVISER

If you are going to pay an adviser, *follow his advice promptly.* He may recommend a stock selling for $20 that pays a $1.00 dividend. If you wait "just to make sure," and the price reaches $22, you have lost a 10 per cent gain and seen the yield drop from 5 per cent to 4½ per cent. This wait-and-see attitude indicates lack of confidence in your adviser and so you are really wasting your money; find another adviser in whom you do have confidence.

You should judge your adviser on his *total* performance over a period of time, say a year or more, and not on the basis of one or two issues for three or four months. Naturally you don't want to lose on any of your investments, but you can afford—and should probably expect—an occasional loss if most of your securities perform well under your adviser's guidance.

Also evaluate your adviser on the basis of *your instructions.*

If you told him you wanted income, don't complain because there is little appreciation. And don't complain if you asked for growth and there is little or no income. Instead, compare your portfolio results, in the light of your instructions, with the general market over the same period of time.

Don't hesitate to question your portfolio manager. After all, the investments are yours, you are paying him, and you have a right to know what is going on. Keep in mind that you may not hear from him as often as from your broker because his fee is based on portfolio value and not on trading commissions.

Again, let me say your investment adviser is not infallible but he should be able to help you lose less in a down market and make more in an up market. Therefore, once you decide to get full-time help, don't put it off until "the market is right."

PART THREE

Techniques of Investing

CHAPTER TEN

Your Own Investment Ideas

WHAT YOUR DAILY EXPERIENCE CAN SUGGEST

The investment community has ascribed a certain mystique to security analysts and their investment recommendations. Yet there is no reason why your selections of stocks can't be every bit as good as theirs if you use their approach. The basis of their method is to be constantly looking for good stocks *before* anyone has expressed great interest in buying them. Don't wait until you have the money to invest and then start looking.

Inspiration for the analysts' recommendations may come from sources that are just as available to you, but you probably have never recognized them as a starting point for selecting your own investments.

THE HOUSEWIFE EVALUATES PRODUCTS

Consider the variety of products bought for the home and immediately put to the test. With a new product, a company won't know for weeks how well it is being received and only then will pass out the good news to the analysts—or try to bury the bad news. As a housewife, you not only buy the product but can also judge how other consumers accept it. They are creating the news the company and the stock analysts have to wait for; so who is in the better position to assess developing trends? You have long been aware of product acceptance, but have you ever considered it as an investment tool?

THE BUSINESSWOMAN EVALUATES

Regardless of what business you are in, salesmen are constantly soliciting orders from your company for their products. If any of them has a revolutionary product available, you can be sure your purchasing agent will learn of it. Tell him or her that you are interested in hearing about, and getting an appraisal of, these new products right away—such things as a new process for color printing, the pocket calculator, the erasing typewriter. This early notice may well lead you directly to a worth-while investment.

Don't forget to check the many trade publications that flow into offices of all types. Most feature new products or processes which are just being introduced and could become highly profitable. A few minutes spent during the lunch hour could develop many good ideas for investment.

If you spot something new that looks good, you are in a perfect position to evaluate it. All you have to do is check with someone in your company—possibly an expert—who would normally be interested in this particular product or service.

THE TRAVELER EVALUATES

Whether you travel on business or pleasure, you will do well to keep your eyes open for investment possibilities. If you were among the first to visit Disneyland, you undoubtedly enjoyed it, but did you also consider it as an investment possibility? Overseas you may have noticed the price and quality of a French wine or Italian shoes or Japanese TV sets, and been impressed with their export possibilities. A call to the United States consulate will get you the information about who may be importing them at home. Upon your return you can check further on the importers as investment possibilities.

If the logic of this approach to finding investment ideas escapes you, consider Tropicana orange juice. When it came on the market you may have decided to try it and then discovered not only that it had everything claimed for it but that your friends and other shoppers were delighted with it. You might have checked acceptance further with the store manager. If he too reported favorably, you could have arranged to buy the stock as soon as it became available in 1969. A $600 investment would have been worth about $6,000 in 1972. Rubbermaid Corporation, maker of what it calls "kitchen organizers," is another example. The price of the stock in the sixties was as low as 2½. Consumer acceptance and increased profits drove the stock price up to 50 by 1973.

In the dual role of shopper and investor, you are among the first to observe whether pantyhose, knitted fabrics, a food franchise like Kentucky Fried Chicken, or various other new products and services are catching the public's fancy. A stock analyst may wait weeks to get this same information. The next time you see something new—hula hoop, ready-made pancake batter, or egg substitute—don't just consider whether or not you want it. Consider whether it will be highly profitable to the company that makes it, and consequently provide a good investment for you.

END PRODUCT OR MACHINES?

When you see something new that you think might be successful, don't conclude that an investment in the end product is your only option. Take knitted fabrics. When they were introduced, woven fabrics dominated the market; now knitted fabrics do. A little thought would have indicated that the knits would create a big demand for knitting machines instead of looms. Thus your consumer approach opens up another opportunity for a good investment besides the end product.

Not long ago Sears, Roebuck & Co. heavily promoted a new product—an appliance to compact garbage without odor. If you had suspected wide consumer acceptance, you might have considered buying Sears stock. However, this was just one of Sears' many items; its success or failure would make little impact on profits. On the other hand, this might be the only product of the company that manufactured it; its success could make a fortune for the company. Your investment in the manufacturing company could in turn become highly profitable.

In retrospect, when evaluating products and services as a consumer, you could have profited by a number of them. It will pay you now to evaluate as an investor.

OPPORTUNITIES IN THE NEWS

The next time you read the paper or listen to the news broadcast and react pro or con, review the facts. Consider the news as an investor—what opportunity does this information present? You may or may not approve of a tremendous grain deal with a foreign country but, as an investor, what are the implications for you? Grain must be transported by rail, barge, and ship and stored in elevators: any firm involved in this phase of the deal might be profitable.

What about next year's crops? Doubtless farmers will increase their grain planting. This could mean increased demand for fertilizer, seed, and farm machinery. Any one of these may profit from the deal and be a good investment. Consider also the region providing the grain for export. Perhaps there is a chain of furniture stores or supermarkets there that will benefit from increased regional prosperity and so be good investments. In just one news report, several opportunities may present themselves for your study.

EFFECT OF APPROPRIATIONS

Any time the federal government passes a large appropriations bill to support a single project, there are possibilities. If a bill is passed to build public schools, consider the specialized equipment that must be purchased—chalkboards, desks, clocks, fire alarms for classrooms; cafeteria, library, and gymnasium equipment . . .

If an appropriation is made to build hospitals on a massive scale, a trip to an existing hospital will give you a good idea of the products that will be required—beds, wheel chairs, crutches, and sophisticated scientific machines.

If mass transit is given huge government support, bus, subway, and railroad-car manufacturers will benefit; so too the makers of equipment that goes into the vehicles and into the systems themselves. In each case various industries and companies will get increased business that may create good investments for you.

Then there are situations where little or no tax money is

involved. A bill is passed requiring every automobile to have seat belts; no tax money is spent. At the rate of a million cars and five passengers per car, an immediate market is created for five million seat belts. An investment in their manufacture has been most profitable.

Anti-pollution bills didn't include tremendous appropriations, but they created a lot of business for manufacturers of pollution controls. An investment in just about any one of them—General Signal, Wheelabrator-Frye, Zurn Industries—was profitable. Emphasis on mine safety may have the same result. These are just a few examples of government news that might have prompted you to make worth-while investments in the past. Who knows what future appropriations or laws will bring?

CONVENTION TOPICS

It's easy to ignore a newspaper article about a union or Chamber of Commerce or other professional group holding a convention. As an investor it will be worth while for you to know that a union is proposing employer-paid dental care, the Chamber of Commerce is urging new school bus safety equipment, or architects are extolling a new building insulation. You may learn of a developing trend that could be very profitable.

At a medical convention the principal subject may have been arthritis, and researchers from various drug firms may have given lectures. It may strike you that one man or one firm is far ahead of the others, and possibly on the verge of a drug breakthrough. A small investment in the drug firm might be the equivalent of an earlier investment in aspirin or the birth control pill. Don't just think what the drug means to the arthritic; carry through to what it can mean to you as an investor.

BAD NEWS?

As you check good news for investments, don't overlook the bad. A flood or a hurricane can put a crimp in insurance profits. Closing the Suez Canal may have helped shipbuilders, but it had a bad effect on oil companies. An overabundance of a product, such as sulphur at one time, can lead to price cutting and lower profits for the companies affected. Maybe the bad news will prompt you to sell one of your stocks and thus improve the performance of your portfolio.

COMPANY VS. INDUSTRY

This approach to investing gives you ideas on *industries* that may be on their way up. However, you have to invest in a *company*, not in an entire industry. Two approaches can narrow your search for a company. You can call your broker and discuss your conclusions for the industry. He can then recommend a specific company. Don't press him for a fast recommendation, for he will probably have to go to his research department for current information. If his firm has closely followed your particular industry, he may have access to reports on several companies that you can study as a basis for a selection.

THOMAS' REGISTER

The alternative is a do-it-yourself approach requiring a little more time and effort. At your public library you will find *Thomas' Register* in several volumes. In one, every conceivable product is included and each is followed by a list of manufacturers. Another volume lists manufacturers followed by their products. You may find under bicycles the XYZ Corporation and the ABC Corporation. When you check the XYZ Corporation, you may find they don't list bicycles as a *principal* product. But the ABC Corporation may list bicycles as their *only* product. With XYZ the product isn't important to their operation, while to ABC it is all-important. If bicycles are going to be in big demand because of the high price of gas, you can easily see which company's earnings will be more favorably affected.

STANDARD & POOR'S SECURITY REPORTS

Regardless of how many companies you select that might profit from the news you have analyzed, you need to know more about each. Your broker, bank trust department, and many libraries subscribe to Standard & Poor's *Security Reports* in addition to the S & P *Stock Guide* described in Chapter Eleven. The *Security Reports* consist of two-page capsulized reports on each company listed on the New York and American

Stock exchanges and many companies whose stocks are traded Over-the-Counter.

These reports, revised quarterly, will bring you up to date on such items as company sales, long-term and near-term business prospects, as well as developments that may affect future profitability. You will also find data on past earnings, dividends, stock prices, and financial information. If there are any unfavorable factors, these too are reported. You may see a statement to the effect that profits declined last year because of the cost of starting up a new factory or a foreign government expropriated property of the company.

A comparison of reports for the companies you are considering may well eliminate all but one or two. At this point you have done considerable research on your own and you can now intelligently discuss companies with your broker to arrive at a wise decision. All this is not as time-consuming as you may think, and, considering the money involved and the length of time you will own the stock, it is well worth your while.

THINK INVESTMENTS

At first, as a serious investor, you will do well to set aside a definite time to ponder news and events from the point of view of buying. When you read the news you will have to make a decided effort to *divorce your personal reaction from your investment analysis*. Once the habit to think investing is established, you will find hours to indulge in it—riding to work, waiting for people late for their appointments, while vacuuming rugs, waiting for the kids to come home from school . . . Don't be discouraged if after a week of this approach you haven't come up with a hot investment idea to research further. In the course of a year you don't need one good idea every week.

This method of finding investments is hardly recommended for those who will risk making a fortune overnight by getting in and out of the market. Rather it is for the investor who wants to buy stock in a good company for the long term without worrying about hour-to-hour or day-to-day fluctuations in prices. This is for the investor who wants to sleep well at night.

Start now to relate consumer preferences and the news to

investing. For one thing, you will find yourself in a much better position to discuss your broker's recommendations. Rather than blindly following his advice, you can ask relevant questions about a company's prospects in the light of known facts that *you* have evaluated. You may indeed follow your broker's recommendations, but still you will have the satisfaction of knowing that you can monitor them and have some say in their selection.

INVESTMENT CLUBS

If you have doubts about selecting investments in this manner you may want to consider an investment club. These clubs serve their members in a variety of ways. Some merely provide social diversion. The more serious clubs, however, offer a learning experience for the novice and a means for the small investor to pool her resources and knowledge.

You may conclude as a result of your observations or news interpretation that a particular industry should be a worthwhile investment. As a member of an investment club, you have an opportunity to present your views to others with a common interest. If the logic of your views is accepted, you can enlist the help of the other members to study which particular company will be the best investment. On the other hand, some members may point out errors in your logic and thus save you a great deal of work pursuing it further on your own.

The situation may be reversed. You are unable to recognize investment possibilities in the news or your surroundings. Other members will present their thinking and you are then in a position to analyze their logic. If the members approve, you will have to study the companies in an industry and be prepared to discuss them at a subsequent meeting. The stock finally selected for investment will then be the result of not just one person's logic, but of many, and all concerned with a common goal.

An active club can go one step further than the individual in researching an investment. Company spokesmen welcome the opportunity to discuss their company and industry with groups, and these meetings can reveal aspects not apparent in printed reports.

Regardless of whether you have a lot or a little to invest, whether you invest all or only a part of it in the club's portfolio, an investment club can be a big help in the selection of investments. If you are unable to find one through your friends, check with the manager of your brokerage firm.

CHAPTER ELEVEN

Evaluating Stocks

WHICH STOCK IS FOR YOU?

It may strike you as contradictory that the same stock can be evaluated as a good buy by one investor and bad by another. The purpose of evaluating a stock is to determine whether it will achieve *your* objective. If you are a conservative investor looking for safety of principal and income, you will look at a stock in a quite different light from the speculative investor who wants fast growth with little regard for income. Always keep in mind what you want a stock to do for *you* when you try to evaluate it.

SAFETY AND LIQUIDITY

When you open a savings account, chances are you will select a bank that pays high interest and insures your deposit with the Federal Deposit Insurance Corporation up to the maximum of $40,000. The F.D.I.C. also guarantees that you can withdraw your principal at any time. As a conservative investor, you might well look at investments from the same point of view—how to get your money out if you need it.

The only way you can sell your stock is to find another investor willing to buy it—a business normally handled by your broker. (Disregard for the moment how much the other investor will pay for your stock.) Your first requirement is that there will *always be a buyer.*

BIG OR LITTLE COMPANIES?

You improve your chances of finding a buyer if a company has issued a *large* number of shares—a million or more. If the stock is selling for only $10, the million shares represent a $10 million investment. Of necessity, then, you would have a good many shareholders who would be potential buyers of additional shares. These shareholders also create market interest in the company by discussing it with their brokers and other investors. This market interest tends to create more potential buyers of your shares.

The second argument in favor of a lot of shares in the hands of investors—referred to as the *float*—is that large institutional investors become potential buyers. They are the mutual funds, bank trust departments, retirement funds, insurance companies, etc., with huge sums to invest. They are faced with two problems—they want to invest in a reasonable number of *different* companies and, for reasons of their own, they don't want to become major stockholders in any one of them. Therefore they avoid companies with relatively few shares outstanding. If you hold stock in a small company, it follows that you have eliminated a considerable number of potential buyers of your shares.

When large investors buy a lot of stock in one company, the news usually appears in the papers. The stock may be included in the daily list of most actively traded stocks. This list is printed in the financial section of your newspaper. Or there will be news that a large block of stock was traded by a certain broker. Such information tends to create additional investor interest in a particular security. A small company can't develop this type of interest and consequent potential buyers.

To be sure of readily turning your investment into cash—*liquidity*—buy shares in a company having several hundred thousand shares or more of stock that is actively traded. This information is shown in the daily price quotations in the *Wall Street Journal*, the weekly quotations in Barron's and monthly quotations in your S & P *Stock Guide* (see Figure 6).

CASH VALUE

Once you are sure there are enough buyers, you can concentrate on how much your stock might be worth to them. In other words, if you suddenly require cash and must sell your stock, what are the chances that you will be able to get back your money?

One way is to invest in a company that has been around long enough to have weathered various economic and competitive situations. The *leading companies* in any industry have usually done this and achieved their position through good management and good products. Typical are Procter and Gamble and Coca-Cola. Should a competitor come along with a revolutionary product, established industry leaders are in a position to adjust to the situation with minimum bad effects. A small company in the industry, however, might be put out of business or at least suffer a severe loss of profit and a consequent drop in the market value of its stock.

A case in point was the transistor business a few years ago. When transistors were introduced, a number of small companies started manufacturing them. As technology was developed by the larger companies, competition increased, and many small companies couldn't keep up and eventually failed. Leaders in the industry met the competition successfully and continued in business. Of course the prices of stock of the larger companies were affected by competition, but much less so than that of the small companies.

A current example is the pocket calculator. When this was introduced, many new small companies started making them before some of the leading calculator manufacturers got started. But it wasn't long before old-timers put their greater technical and financial skills to work and became dominant in the pocket calculator business. The smaller companies then began to disappear from the scene.

SHORT TERM VS. LONG TERM

In both cases a *short-term* investment in the newcomers might have made a substantial profit, but it would always have

STANDARD & POOR'S CORPORATION

INDEX	Ticker Symbol	STOCKS NAME OF ISSUE (Call Price of Pfd. Stocks)	Market	Par Val.	Inst. Hold Cos	Inst. Hold Shs. (000)	PRINCIPAL BUSINESS	PRICE RANGE 1960-72 High	1960-72 Low	1973 High	1973 Low	1974 High	1974 Low	Jan. Sales in 100s	January, 1975 Last Sale Or Bid High	Low	Last	% Div. Yield	P-E Ratio
1	DPL	Dayton Pwr & Light	NYS,Bo,Ci,PB	7	65	1066	Elec & gas utility serving	38¼	15¼	25	17¾	21⅜	10⅝	2123	16	12	15¾	10.5	8
2	Pr D	7.48%cm D Pfd ([51]106.965)	NYS([10])	100	28	51	industrialized Dayton and	105	88	102½	94	94½	61	3	66	66	69B	10.8	..
3	Pr E	7.70% cm E Pfd ([52]108)	NYS([10])	100	16	58	agric surrounding area	108	97½	105	94	97	61	9	65	62½	67B	11.5	..
4	Pr F	7.375% cm F Pfd ([53]107.5)	NYS([10])	100	21	62		....	....	100	92½	94½	61	1	63	63	62B	11.9	..
5	Pr G	12.5% cm G Pfd ([54]112)	NYS([10])	100	1	5		....	....	....	....	109	100	17	110¼	102	110½	11.4	..
6	DCL	DCL Inc	ASE,Bo,PB	3⅓¢	2	186	Leasing computer systems	31½	2	3	¼	⅞	¼	141	½	¼	⅜B	...	d
7	DEAN	Dean Foods	OTC	1	..	...	Milk & dairy: food items	34⅜	14	17	12¾	15½	12¼	32	14	12¼	14B	7.9	4
8	DW	Dean Witter Organiz'n	NYS,PS	1	1	30	Major firm in securities indus	32	15½	18⅜	6¼	8½	4¼	908	8⅜	5¾	8	5.0	8
9	DBNN	Debron Corp	OTC	5	1	.4	Steel fabricator	25⅞	7	13¾	8⅝	12½	7¼	65	8¾	7¼	8½B	9.4	5
10	DDCC	Decision Data Comp	OTC	10¢	4	235	Computer auxil eq:leas'g	50	14½	39½	5½	13½	2¾	1333	6¼	4⅝	6¼B	...	45
11	DCOR	Decorator Indus	OTC	No	1	2	Mfr & dstr of draperies	23½	2⅜	7¼	2⅜	4⅜	1¼	131	2¼	1⅝	2¼B	8.9	5
12	DE	Deere & Co	NYS,Bo,Ci,De,MW,PB,PS	1	236	6133	Mfr farm eq: constr mchy	48	9⁹⁄₁₆	65½	35⅝	53⅞	27¾	7806	43⅛	37⅛	38⅜	4.7	7
13	DEJ A	DeJur-Amsco Cl A	ASE	1	1	3	Office eqp: amateur movie eq	25⅞	⅞	5⅛	2¼	4⅛	2⅜	12	4⅛	3½	3⅞B	...	d
14	DKLBB	DEKALB AgResearch[55]	OTC	No	26	495	Hybrid seed: poultry: oil	57½	6⅛	63	37½	51¼	23	5941	37¾	32	33¾B	0.6	18
15	DLI	Del Laboratories	ASE	1	..	...	Makes toiletries & cosmetics	24½	3½	13¾	5⅞	8⅝	4½	78	5½	5	5¼B	3.8	4
16	DLHI	Delhi Int'l Oil	OTC	10¢	4	154	Explore, devel oil, gas lands	17⅛	4⅝	7¾	3½	5⅝	1	348	2⅝	1½	2½B	...	d
17	DEW	Delmarva Pwr & Lt	NYS,Bo,PB	3⅜	54	1274	Elec & gas: Delaware, Md, Va	32¼	15⅛	17⅜	13	15⅛	7⅛	3764	11⅜	9	11⅛	10.8	6
18	DEL	Del Monte	NYS,Bo,Ho,PB,PS	2½	17	651	Largest packer fruits & vegs	38⅜	11¾	23⅞	15¾	24⅜	16	1727	25¼	20⅝	24⅞	5.2	6
19	DELM	Del Monte Properties	OTC	2½	4	34	Sand:resort/recreation:R.E.	29	10	16¾	10¼	18	6½	578	7⅝	6½	7⅝B	5.8	5
20	DAL	Delta Air Lines	NYS,Bo,De,MW,PB,PS	3	144	4769	Domestic, Caribbean system	65¾	1⅜	68⅜	35¼	56⅛	27⅞	8681	32⅛	25⅜	31⅜	1.9	7
21	DCAL	Delta California Indus	OTC	50¢	..	...	Calif-Nevada trucking	12½	8½	12	3¼	5½	4	59	5¾	5½	5¾B	4.3	6
22	DLA	Delta Corp of Amer	ASE,Bo,PB,PS	10¢	2	165	Contract financ'g: mobile hms	35⅜	3¾	7⅜	½	2¼	¼	324	⅞	⅜	¾	...	d
23	DTL	Deltec Int'l Ltd ADR	#NYS,Bo,TS	1	1	50	Invest/merch bank'g:food,R.E.	30⅝	4⅜	10⅛	6⅛	8	1⅝	355	4½	1⅞	3½	...	d
24	DLT	Deltona Corp	NYS,MW,PB,PS	1	11	298	Florida land developer	74⅝	4⅛	24¼	6⅛	9⅝	2¾	722	5⅝	3½	5⅝	...	13
25	DTN	Deltown Foods	ASE	1	..	...	Dairy pdts: NY-NJ metr area	28⅞	4½	20¼	6¾	13	4½	80	7	5⅜	6⅞	7.9	6
26	DELX	De Luxe Check Print	OTC	1	26	486	Prints checks, other bk forms	41¾	3¼	41¼	30	35	12¼	3964	25¾	22½	24½B	2.0	18
27	DFUR	Delwood Furniture	OTC	1	..	...	Mfr home,office,school furn	16	11½	12¾	2½	7	1¾	142	3	1⅞	3B	...	3
28	DENIF	Denison Mines Ltd	OTC,MS,TS	1	30	867	Uranium: oil: cement	86⅞	8¼	52¾	28½	56¼	34	97	43¾	35¼	43¼B	◆3.2	16
29	DSN	Dennison Mfg.	NYS,Bo	5	15	311	Gen'l stationery supplies,	80	7½	38⅜	17⅝	22½	10¼	485	16¼	12⅞	15¼	5.9	4
30	Pr	$1 cm Cv Pfd ([59]24)1/2vtg	NYS	10	4	23	custom & specialty papers	60¼	12½	28	16	19	10¾	16	14	11	14	7.1	..
31	DEN	Denny's Inc	NYS,Bo,MW,PB,PS	1	14	1344	Coffee & donut shops	52⅝	1½	20¾	7⅜	13⅞	5⅞	3373	10¼	6⅜	9⅞	2.0	8
32	DTZ	Den-Tal-Ez,Inc	ASE,PB	1	18	182	Dental eq: chair, stool, tray	62½	4½	57⅜	13¾	16¼	5⅜	913	9½	7⅝	9¼	2.2	6
33	DSP	Dentsply Int'l	NYS,Bo	1	24	386	Dental/optical eq:optic strs	36⅜	9	29¾	16¼	29½	20¼	1118	27⅛	23	26⅛	3.1	13
34	DENV	Denver Real Estate Inv	OTC	No	2	107	Real estate investment trust	15¾	8⅛	9	6⅝	7¼	5⅝	131	7	5¾	7B	†10.0	10
35	DEP	Depositors Corp	ASE	6¼	..	...	Bank holdg: Maine banks	38½	19⅞	21¾	16⅞	20⅛	13¼	38	16⅛	14¾	16	9.0	4
36	DRO	Dero Indus[61]	ASE	5¢	..	...	Leisure time, shoe, fabric	35⅞	2¼	3⅛	⅜	¾	⅜	Trading halted ASE					
37	DRI	De Rose Indus	ASE	No	..	...	Mfr mobile homes for whlsle	16⅛	4	5⅛	1	2½	⅜	84	1⅜	½	1⅜	...	d
38	DPH	Deseret Pharmaceut'l	NYS,Bo	50¢	18	525	Medical & surgical devices	31⅝	2	34	18¼	25	4½	1138	9⅛	5¾	8⅜	...	16
39	DJI	Designcraft Jewel Ind	ASE	2¢	..	...	Gold rings,earrings:watches	38¼	7¼	16⅞	3⅝	5⅝	⅞	46	1⅜	1	1⅛B	...	d
40	DSO	DeSoto, Inc	NYS	1	9	414	Paints, furniture, TV cabinets	42½	7	16¼	8	11⅞	4	745	7⅜	5⅞	7	8.6	6
41	DTRX	Detrex Chemical Ind	OTC	2	3	14	Metal,laundry chem cleaners	23¾	3⅞	8⅝	6½	10⅜	6½	87	8⅞	8⅛	8⅞B	9.0	3
42	DTUN	Detroit & Can. Tunnel	OTC	5	..	...	Toll tunnel, Detroit River	20¼	12½	17	13¼	14¼	8¾	31	9¾	8¾	9½B	13.7	7

Uniform Footnote Explanations—See Page 1. Other: [51]To 4-30-79,scale to $103.225 in'84. [52]To 4-1-78, scale to $101 in '86. [53]To 6-1-78, scale to $101 in'88. [54]To 10-31-84, scale to $101 in'90. [55]Cl B,non-vtg. [56]®$1.28,'73. [57]®$3.12,'74. [58]®$1.44,'73. [59]To 5-31-75, scale to $22 in'77. [60]Fiscal Jul,'70 & prior. [61]ASE trad'g halted Oct 10,'74. [62]Excl.$0.44 gain on disp.. [63]®$1.34,'73. [64]Approx 1% '74 non-taxable.

COMMON AND PREFERRED STOCKS

INDEX	Some Divs. Ea. Yr. Since	DIVIDENDS — Latest Payment — Per $	Date	Ex. Div.	$ So Far 1975	Total Ind. Rate	$ Paid 1974	FINANCIAL POSITION — Mil-$ — Cash & Equiv.	Curr. Assets	Curr. Liabs.	Balance Sheet Date	CAPITALIZATION — Long Term Debt Mil-$	Shs. 000 — Pfd.	Com.	Ended	$ Per Shr—EARNINGS—$ Per Shr — Years — 1970	1971	1972	1973	1974	INTERIM EARNINGS OR REMARKS — Period	$—Per Share—$ 1973	INDEX
1	1919	Q0.41½	3-1-75	2-3	0.41½	1.66	1.66	4.73	64.9	98.8	9-30-74	*394.	*1079	*13726	Dc	2.15	2.07	2.15	1.87	P1.89			1
2	1969	Q1.87	3-1-75	2-3	1.87	7.48	7.48	...	...	...		....	150	...	Dc	59.05	43.04	46.84	32.61	....			2
3	1971	Q1.92½	3-1-75	2-3	1.92½	7.70	7.70	Redm restr(7.70%) to 4-1-78				....	200	...	Dc	....	43.04	46.84	32.61	....			3
4	1973	Q1.84⅜	3-1-75	2-3	1.84⅜	7.37½	7.37½	Redm rstr(7.375%) to 6-1-78				....	250	...	Dc	....	....	....	32.61	....			4
5	1974	Q3.12½	3-1-75	2-3	3.12½	12.50	1.111	Redm restr(12.5%)to 11-1-84				....	250	...	Dc	....	....	....	....	....	SF 12,500	$100 fr'79	5
6	.....	None Paid			....	Nil	....	Equity per shr $2.87			12-31-73	32.2	...	3268	Dc	0.48	0.93	d7.14	d1.45	....	9 Mo Sep	0.31	6
7	1941	Q0.27½	1-3-75	12-6	0.27½	1.10	1.02½	2.02	37.6	26.5	12-31-73	9.66	...	885	Dc	2.15	2.26	1.03	2.31	....	9 Mo Sep	1.33	7
8	1972	Q0.10	2-1-75	1-6	0.10	0.40	0.40	Equity per shr $15.80			8-31-74	24.0	...	4180	Au	0.39	2.87	2.90	0.75	□0.91	3 Mo Nov	0.40	8
9	1939	Q0.20	3-10-75	1-27	0.20	0.80	0.80	1.90	30.4	14.6	12-31-73	0.56	...	1097	Dc	1.22	□1.00	Δ1.40	2.00	....	9 Mo Sep	1.27	9
10	.....	None Since Public			....	Nil	....	1.38	15.2	11.8	12-1-73	2.01	...	3735	Nv	d0.61	d0.96	d0.94	d0.25	....	9 Mo Aug	d0.27	10
11	1967	Q0.05	12-27-74	12-4	....	0.20	0.20	1.27	6.74	2.89	2-2-74	2.18	...	1595	Ja	0.37	□0.51	0.47	0.61	....	9 Mo Oct	0.51	11
12◆	1937	Q0.45	4-1-75	2-25	0.85	1.80	1.50	55.5	1475	698.	10-31-74	216.	...	29669	Oc	1.56	2.15	3.82	5.75	5.55			12
13◆	.....	3%Stk	6-29-71	6-9	....	Nil	....	2.12	6.26	0.76	12-31-73	....	...	p560	Dc	0.45	0.39	0.40	d0.15	....	9 Mo Sep	0.09	13
14◆	1937	Q0.05	12-17-74	11-26	....	0.20	0.20	28.7	149.	77.7	8-31-74	17.6	...	±12308	Au	0.74	0.92	1.13	1.50	1.88	3 Mo Nov	0.03	14
15	1973	Q0.05	3-28-75	2-24	0.05	0.20	0.20	1.41	11.5	2.98	12-31-73	5.84	...	1186	Dc	□0.74	□1.13	1.23	∫[56]1.40	....	9 Mo Sep	1.17	15
16	.....	None Paid			....	Nil	....	0.71	3.39	17.8	12-31-73	21.8	...	4381	Dc	d0.30	□d0.38	d0.46	d0.52	....	9 Mo Sep	d0.18	16
17	1921	Q0.30	1-31-75	1-2	0.30	1.20	1.20	11.5	77.7	94.0	10-31-74	*378.	1050	*16474	Dc	1.48	1.71	1.77	1.79	P1.73			17
18	1940	Q0.32½	2-15-75	1-13	0.32½	1.30	1.22½	60.7	414.	186.	5-31-74	145.	...	12007	My	□1.52	1.77	1.92	2.16	[57]3.26	6 Mo Nov	1.45	18
19	1945	Q0.11	12-1-74	11-8	....	0.44	0.44	0.79	4.97	2.53	12-31-73	4.30	216	1453	Dc	0.89	1.23	1.48	[58]1.50	....	9 Mo Sep	0.95	19
20	1949	Q0.15	3-1-75	2-3	0.15	0.60	0.60	44.4	137.	161.	9-30-74	373.	...	19879	Je	2.33	1.57	1.68	3.32	4.56	6 Mo Dec	2.03	20
21	1971	Q0.06¼	12-31-74	11-27	....	0.25	0.25	2.21	11.1	8.56	12-31-73	11.6	...	1415	Dc	Δ0.12	Λ1.18	•Δ1.39	0.64	....	9 Mo Sep	0.35	21
22◆	.....	5%Stk	5-15-70	4-29	....	Nil	....	Equity per shr $3.95			12-31-73	....	...	1946	Dc	0.71	Δd0.17	0.14	d0.50	....	9 Mo Sep	d0.27	22
23	1973	0.10	9-5-74	8-12	....	Nil	0.30	73.1	...	...	9-30-74	....	...	4520	Sp	d1.12	□1.71	Δ1.34	•Δ1.58	d2.22	3 Mo Dec	0.22	23
24		None since 1954			....	Nil	....	Equity per shr $18.42			12-31-73	193.	...	3695	Dc	1.15	1.58	2.20	∫1.57	....	9 Mo Sep	1.27	24
25	1970	Q0.13½	3-1-75	2-5	0.13½	0.54	0.54	3.05	17.5	10.8	12-31-73	7.06	...	688	Dc	Λ1.53	Λ1.78	Δ1.94	1.14	....	9 Mo Sep	0.47	25
26◆	1921	Q0.12	12-2-74	11-14	....	0.48	0.469	12.7	40.4	18.7	12-31-73	1.90	...	11890	Dc	0.79	0.91	1.05	1.17	P1.33			26
27	.....	None Since Public			....	Nil	....	1.00	20.3	5.62	12-31-73	5.20	...	4000	Dc	0.75	0.91	1.16	1.19	....	9 Mo Sep	0.96	27
28	1959	gQ0.35	12-13-74	11-27	....	1.40	g1.40	4.94	24.1	29.3	j12-31-73	10.4	...	4568	Dc	1.82	□2.11	1.73	2.15	ΔP2.69			28
29	1942	Q0.22½	12-10-74	11-1	....	0.90	0.90	3.80	81.5	24.3	12-31-73	20.8	483	2510	Dc	1.82	2.51	3.03	∫3.50	E3.60	9 Mo Sep	2.53	29
30	1967	Q0.25	12-10-74	11-1	....	1.00	1.00	Conv into 0.75 shrs common				....	464	...	Dc	10.70	14.84	18.84	21.61	....			30
31	1964	0.10	1-2-75	12-3	0.10	0.20	0.12	n/a	26.8	25.4	9-30-74	33.7	402	6462	Je	0.81	0.40	0.52	0.75	∫1.12	6 Mo Dec	0.59	31
32◆	1973	Q0.05	1-31-75	1-6	0.05	0.20	0.20	1.05	11.4	1.56	12-31-73	2.32	...	1343	Dc	[60]0.74	1.14	1.42	∫1.24	....	9 Mo Sep	1.11	32
33◆	1900	Q0.20	3-4-75	2-7	0.20	0.80	0.76	4.36	43.0	16.5	12-31-73	5.38	...	4426	Dc	1.03	1.04	1.20	1.55	E1.95	9 Mo Sep	1.17	33
34	1961	†0.25	1-24-75	1-9	†0.25	0.70	0.60	Equity per shr $8.85			9-30-74	27.4	...	1091	Dc	0.61	0.47	0.46	□0.51	....	9 Mo Sep	□0.34	34
35	1966	Q0.36	1-23-75	1-6	0.36	1.44	1.28	Book Value $25.65			9-30-74	9.00	...	707	Dc	Δ3.14	Λ2.71	Δ2.24	□3.12	P□4.16			35
36◆	.....	h....	7-11-72	7-18	....	Nil	....	0.11	2.25	2.18	8-31-73	1.84	...	1099	Au	Δ1.51	□d0.05	□d3.36	□[62]d0.75	....	9 Mo May	Δd0.55	36
37◆	.....	None Paid			....	Nil	....	1.24	5.41	1.29	12-31-73	0.81	...	1446	Dc	0.77	0.61	0.16	0.04	....	9 Mo Sep	0.18	37
38◆	1973	0.06¼	9-26-74	8-20	....	Nil	0.25	0.36	17.9	10.2	11-30-74	....	...	2836	Au	Δ0.17	0.47	0.81	1.11	∫0.69	3 Mo Nov	0.26	38
39	.....	None Since Public			....	Nil	....	1.27	21.6	7.14	2-28-74	8.90	...	878	Fb	[8]0.40	Λ0.69	0.80	0.91	....	9 Mo Nov	0.75	39
40	1957	Q0.15	1-17-75	12-26	0.15	0.60	0.60	6.15	97.0	64.8	12-31-73	10.1	...	5414	Dc	0.96	0.83	1.03	1.53	....	9 Mo Sep	1.23	40
41	1947	Q0.20	12-31-74	12-11	....	0.80	0.62	2.21	13.6	5.19	12-31-73	3.70	206	665	Dc	□d0.27	d0.09	Δ•0.68	[63]1.57	....	9 Mo Sep	1.10	41
42	1941	Q0.32½	1-31-75	1-15	0.32½	1.30	[64]1.30	1.31	1.78	0.32	10-31-74	....	....	727	Oc	1.50	1.43	1.55	1.40	1.31			42

◆ Stock Splits & Divs By Line Reference Index [12]2-for-1,'72. [13]Adj to 3%,'71. [14]20%,'71:2-for-1,'72. [22]Adj for 5%,'70:5-for-4, Mar & Oct'71. [26]100%,'71:'72. [32]2-for-1,'71. [33]3-for-2,'70:'73. [36]Adj to 5%, '71. [37]10%, '70. [38]2-for-1,'72:Adj for 4%,'72.

6. *Standard & Poor's* Stock Guide

been subject to sudden collapse. An investment in one of the old-time industry leaders might not have produced an initial overnight gain but it also wouldn't have produced any overnight drop.

If you are inclined to speculate and trade a great deal more than a conservative investor, you will no doubt look for these small companies that have a revolutionary new product and relatively few shares of stock. Your theory will be that the new product will create a big demand for the small supply of shares and the price of the shares will rise substantially. If this happens, you should sell at a *reasonable profit* before this glamor stock drops in price.

There is an adage that the Bulls make money, the Bears make money, but the Hogs never! The speculative approach is better left to the sophisticated investor who may be able to take a big risk and perhaps lose a lot of money without feeling it too much.

If your objective is safety, check with your broker before you buy. He can give you an indication of how volatile—how fast the ups and downs—of your contemplated stock has been. If you have to sell suddenly, you don't want to own a stock that was way above your cost last week and way below it this week.

THE HIGH AND LOW PRICE

Your broker can also give you the high and low prices of a stock over the past twelve months or more; so can your *Stock Guide*. But don't settle for this information alone, because it really doesn't tell you enough. Also, there is a subconscious tendency to conclude that the low price was a year ago and the high price only recently. Ask your broker for a *graph* of the stock's price over the past year or longer. The two graphs shown in Figures 7 and 8 make it obvious why the high and the low figures alone don't tell all; the graphs give meaning to the figures.

In both cases there were fluctuations in price, but you can see that Interlake, Inc. showed a generally *improving* price while Milton Bradley Co. did not. If you wanted assurance that you could sell your stock at any time and recoup your investment, on the basis of past performance, Interlake, Inc. would have been safer because the price performance was more uniform. Keep

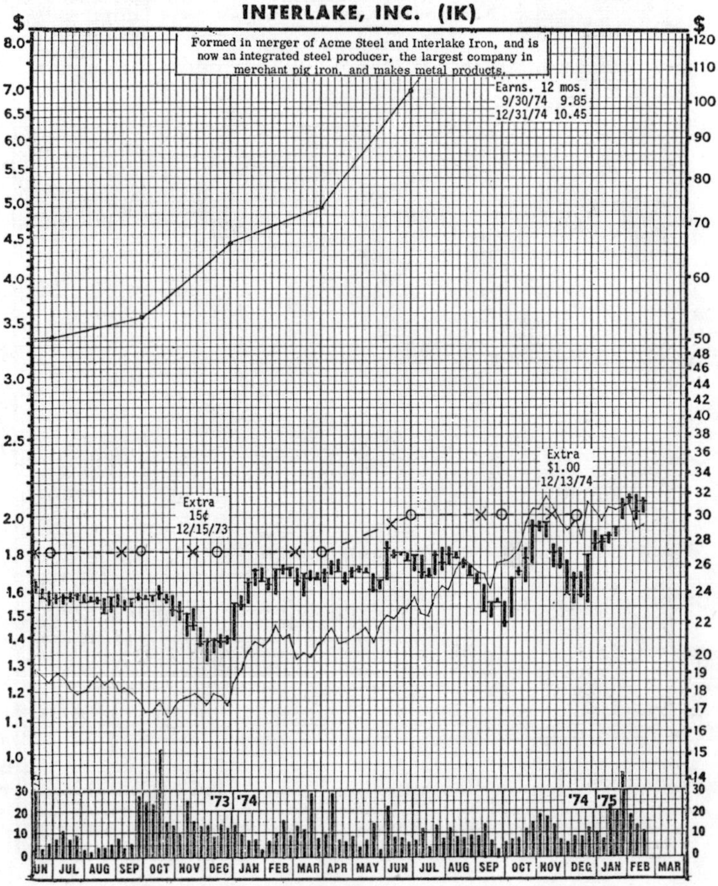

7. *Stock Price, Earnings, and Dividend Graphs*
(COURTESY OF SECURITIES RESEARCH COMPANY)

in mind, however, that past performance is no guarantee for the future.

If you had bought *both* stocks at a high point and been forced to sell at a low point, your loss would have been greater with Milton Bradley Co. than with Interlake, Inc. However, if you are an avid follower of stock prices, a nimble trader, and willing to take risks, you could have made more with Milton Bradley Co. with its short-term ups and downs provided you traded at the right times.

While these graphs show *historical* price patterns, you can

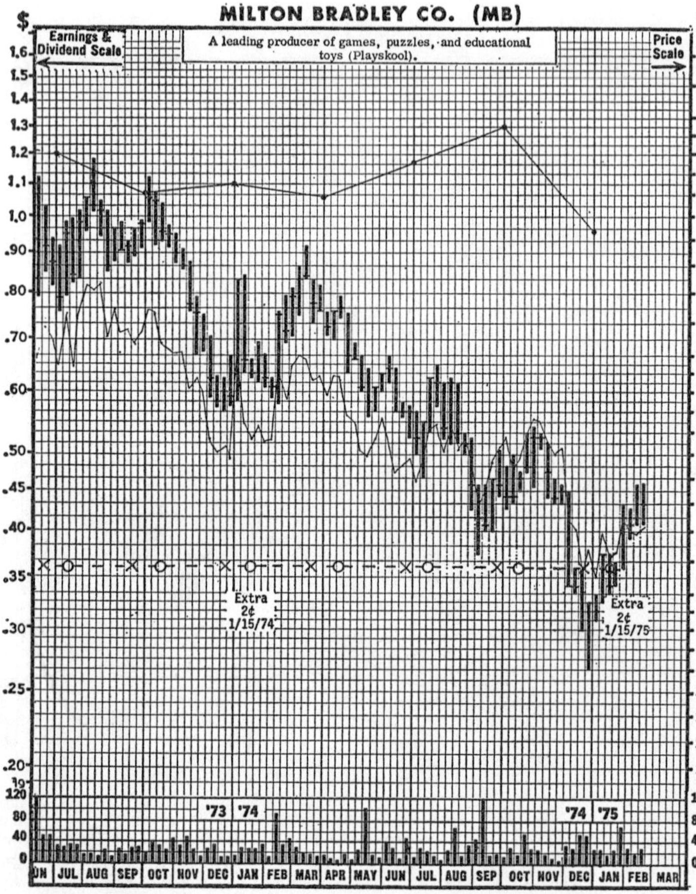

8. Stock Price, Earnings, and Dividend Graphs
(COURTESY OF SECURITIES RESEARCH COMPANY)

derive some confidence in the possibility that these patterns will continue.

EARNINGS—WILL THEY INCREASE?

Bear in mind that when you buy stock in a company you become part owner—and who wants to own a company that doesn't earn a profit? The fact that a company earns a profit in successive years gives your investment a constant value, but *if the value only remains constant*, you might as well open a savings account. If the profits steadily increase in successive years, then your investment will also increase in value. Ask your broker to give you earnings figures over the past several years; if they show a steady increase, you're on the right track. Management has performed well and you can reasonably expect it to continue.

PRICE/EARNINGS RATIO

The next point to consider about a stock is its value, usually expressed as P/E, *price-to-earnings ratio.* This may sound complicated, but it shouldn't because you probably compute other values the same way when you shop.

Suppose you are buying a radio and have to choose between one for $150, with an expected life of five years, and one for $200 with an expected life of eight years. Assuming both will operate for full life expectancy, you divide the $150 by five years; this gives you a cost of $30 per year. Then you divide $200 by eight years and your answer is $25 per year. You might call this a price-to-usage ratio of 30 to 1 and 25 to 1. The $200 radio, you conclude, is a better buy.

As you see, ratio involves dividing one number by another. The *price/earnings ratio* consists of dividing the price per share by the twelve months' earnings per share. Thus a $40 stock (price) which earned $2.00 (earnings) has a price/earnings ratio of 40 divided by 2 or 20 to 1. In shortened form this is referred to as the P/E ratio. Or you may hear it said that the stock is selling at twenty times earnings, another way of saying the same thing.

If you measure a conservative stock like Kraftco by its relative price stability and good yield, then, generally speaking, the stock with a low P/E ratio is more conservative than one with a high P/E ratio. Conversely, a speculative stock with above-average growth and little income like International Flavors & Fragrances may have an extremely high P/E ratio.

There is no specific price-to-earnings ratio that can be classified as a good value. It is all relative. Successful companies in the same industry should have approximately the same P/E ratio; if they don't you will probably find that the company with the higher ratio is more speculative.

Eastman Kodak and Polaroid are examples of this difference in P/E ratios for companies in the same industry. Historically the

P/E ratio for Kodak has been about half that for Polaroid. The yield on Kodak is three times as great as on Polaroid. Over a ten-year period Polaroid rose almost 700 per cent in price compared to 550 per cent in Kodak, but Polaroid has also had more severe ups and downs. Also, during the general market decline in 1970 and 1974, Kodak's market price declined only half as much as Polaroid's. Of the two, Eastman Kodak's lower P/E ratio indicates a somewhat more conservative investment in the photographic industry.

Now let's compare Kodak and General Motors. At the end of 1973 their P/E ratios were twenty-five and six times earnings respectively. General Motors' yield is almost ten times as great, but between 1962 and 1972 the market price increased only 35 per cent compared to Kodak's 550 per cent.

You can see that P/E ratios, though relative, do provide an indication of the speculative nature of a stock. The more you are concerned with good steady income and steady moderate growth, the more you should look for stocks having relatively *low* price/earnings ratios. The P/E ratios are normally included with the more complete listings of stock market quotations found in the *Wall Street Journal*, Barron's, or the S & P *Stock Guide.*

INCOME—WILL IT CONTINUE?

Even if you are looking primarily for income, do follow these various procedures for evaluating a stock; then determine whether the percentage yield meets your needs. Although the current dividend may be satisfactory, the company's board of directors may change it at any time, and you should assure yourself that the likelihood of this happening is slight. So examine earnings records in your *Stock Guide.*

The dividends you expect can only be paid from *current* or from *retained earnings* from previous years. If these earnings drop drastically, the dividend could be skipped or at least reduced. You can easily determine how reliable the dividend is. If the company has been paying a 70-cent dividend and has been earning $1.00, then there is ample money to pay the dividend. In other words, the dividend is well covered. Had the regular dividend been 95 cents or $1.00 in the past, and only $1.00 has been earned, then you should be prepared for a dividend cut or even a temporary suspension.

In late 1970 you may have bought USM Corporation—formerly United Shoe Machinery Company—for about $23 because the yield was about 7 per cent. Unfortunately earnings had already started a serious decline and in the first half of 1971 were no longer large enough to cover the dividend. The third-quarter dividend payment was slashed from 40 cents to 25 cents and the fourth payment to 10 cents. The year 1972 saw a rapid recovery in earnings, but it wasn't until 1973 that management decided to gradually increase the dividend.

Ordinarily a good *income stock* will pay 50 per cent or more of its earnings to shareholders in the form of dividends. A *growth stock* will pay only a small percentage, if any, and retain most of the earnings to finance growth.

WORD OF WARNING

As you become interested in investments and discuss them with friends and acquaintances, you will be sure to be given many tips, touts, and rumors. *Ignore them.* And don't ask just anyone for a stock evaluation. The answer you get is his or her opinion of the stock as it pertains to *his* or *her* investment objective and not to *yours.*

Don't buy a stock on a friendly tipster's recommendation, but don't be afraid to listen and then make your own evaluation. He may have profitably owned his favorite for several years but decide to sell it tomorrow. However, it wouldn't occur to him to tell you of his decision.

When acting on even a professional evaluation, assure yourself that the adviser will be around to tell you *when to sell* your stock and knows you expect him to tell you.

Stock evaluation is a continuing process because earnings, stock price, and dividends all change, and these changes can alter original evaluations.

CHAPTER TWELVE

Record Keeping and Safeguarding Securities

A BOTHER THAT PAYS OFF

Record keeping at best is a chore. But records are a necessary evil, and in the long run they can be a godsend. It isn't important what form you use for your records. What is important is that you not only start records on your investments but keep them up to date and complete.

Several standard record forms are available from your stationery store. Because they include spaces for all the pertinent information, you will probably find them more efficient than trying to make up your own form. Figures 9, 10, and 11 show two styles. Here is the information you will need most:

1. Company name of the security
2. Whether common or preferred stock or bond
3. Date of purchase
4. Certificate number
5. Number of shares or bonds bought or sold
6. Purchase price per share and total value
7. Selling price per share and total value
8. Profit or loss when sold
9. Dividends received
10. Dividend payment dates

Optional Information:

11. Name of agent paying dividend—in case a check is lost
12. Name of transfer agent—who can arrange replacement of a lost certificate for you

13. Name of stockholder—if you are keeping children's records
14. Name of broker who bought or sold for you

Don't put off making entries. Details are too easily forgotten and if, because of illness, somebody else has to take over, the latest information should be available.

IMPORTANCE OF RECORDS

It is not uncommon for an investor to own stock—let's say Atlantic Richfield—which was acquired as a gift or inheritance many years earlier. If this stock is sold, the original cost has to be known for capital gains tax purposes. The problem is that when the original stock was acquired there was no Atlantic Richfield. There was an Atlantic Refining Corporation, a Richfield Oil Corporation, and a Sinclair Oil Company. All of these were combined at different times and on different terms to form today's Atlantic Richfield Corporation. If the year of acquisition is known, the original cost value can usually be estimated fairly accurately, but it is a tedious chore—especially when it has to be done to pay taxes. If you find yourself in this situation, your best starting point for information is *Capital Changes Reporter* or Moody's *Industrial Manual*, probably available at your library. They include all merger and acquisition information, but why not keep your own records!

The *Capital Changes Reporter* can be equally helpful if you come across an old stock certificate and want to know if it has any value.

You will find the dividend record shown in Figures 10 and 11 most helpful at tax time when you have to declare your unearned income. It also provides a double check on whether you have received each dividend.

It's not absolutely necessary that you keep your broker's confirmation of each transaction, but it is easy enough to clip it to the security record or keep it with your canceled checks. You never know when a confirmation might settle a question with the Internal Revenue Service.

When you sell a security and complete your record on it, it's a simple matter to file the record with your canceled checks and bank statements. The importance of *keeping old records*

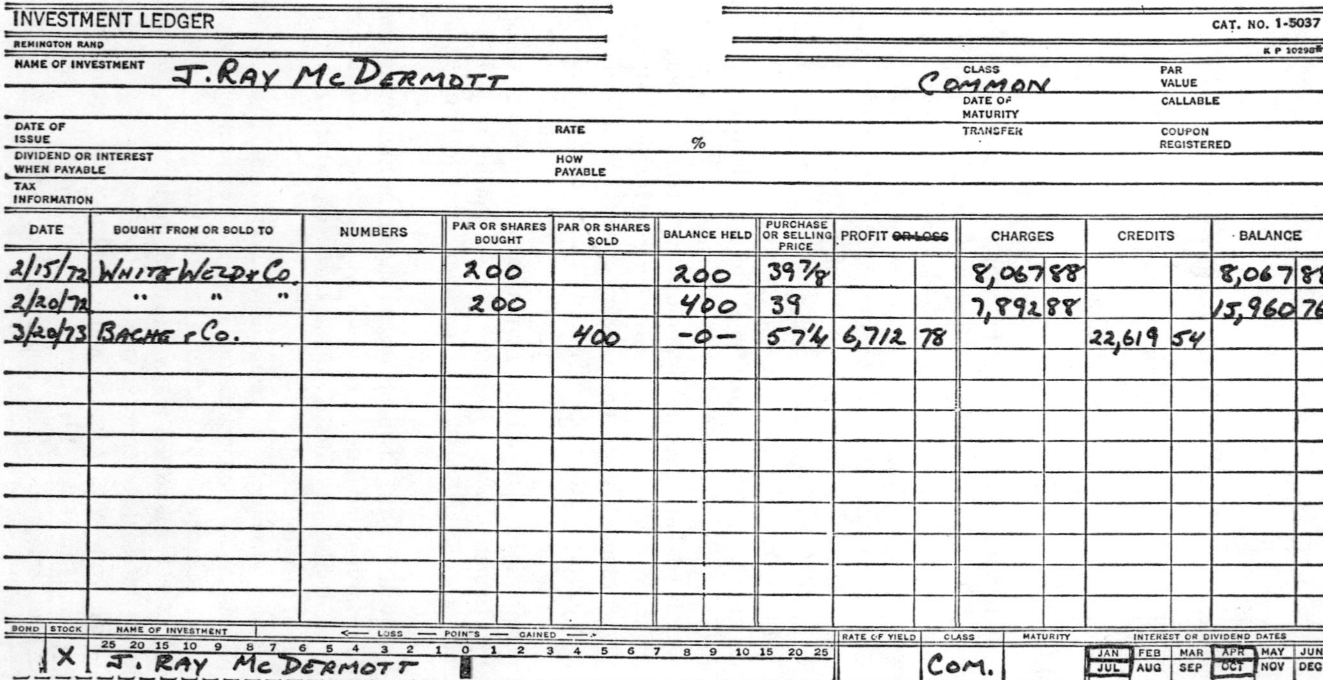

INVESTMENT LEDGER

REMINGTON RAND

CAT. NO. 1-5037

K P 10298*

NAME OF INVESTMENT J. RAY McDERMOTT

CLASS COMMON

PAR VALUE

DATE OF MATURITY

CALLABLE

DATE OF ISSUE

RATE %

TRANSFER

COUPON REGISTERED

DIVIDEND OR INTEREST WHEN PAYABLE

HOW PAYABLE

TAX INFORMATION

DATE	BOUGHT FROM OR SOLD TO	NUMBERS	PAR OR SHARES BOUGHT	PAR OR SHARES SOLD	BALANCE HELD	PURCHASE OR SELLING PRICE	PROFIT ~~OR LOSS~~	CHARGES	CREDITS	BALANCE
2/15/72	WHITE WELD & Co.		200		200	39⅞		8,067 88		8,067 88
2/20/72	" " "		200		400	39		7,892 88		15,960 76
3/20/73	BACHE & Co.			400	-0-	57¼	6,712 78		22,619 54	

BOND	STOCK	NAME OF INVESTMENT	← LOSS — POINTS — GAINED → 25 20 15 10 9 8 7 6 5 4 3 2 1 0 1 2 3 4 5 6 7 8 9 10 15 20 25	RATE OF YIELD	CLASS	MATURITY	INTEREST OR DIVIDEND DATES
	X	J. RAY McDERMOTT			COM.		JAN JUL / FEB AUG / MAR SEP / APR OCT / MAY NOV / JUN DEC

9. *Investment Ledger* (COURTESY OF SPERRY REMINGTON, DIVISION OF SPERRY RAND CORPORATION)

J. RAY McDERMOTT

REMINGTON RAND — DIVIDENDS AND INTEREST RECORD — RRNT-12574 CAT. NO. 1-9138

1972	DATE	RATE	SHARES	AMOUNT			DATE	RATE	SHARES	AMOUNT	
FIRST						FIRST					
SECOND	4/3	.25	400	100	00	SECOND					
THIRD	7/3	.25	400	100	00	THIRD					
FOURTH	10/2	.25	400	100	00	FOURTH					
TOTAL				300	00	TOTAL					

1973	DATE	RATE	SHARES	AMOUNT			DATE	RATE	SHARES	AMOUNT	
FIRST	1/2	.25	400	100	00	FIRST					
SECOND						SECOND					
THIRD						THIRD					
FOURTH						FOURTH					
TOTAL						TOTAL					

	DATE	RATE	SHARES	AMOUNT			DATE	RATE	SHARES	AMOUNT	
FIRST						FIRST					
SECOND						SECOND					
THIRD						THIRD					
FOURTH						FOURTH					
TOTAL						TOTAL					

10. Dividend and Interest Record (COURTESY OF SPERRY REMINGTON, DIVISION OF SPERRY RAND CORPORATION)

STOCKS

COMPANY	Eastman Kodak	KIND OF BUSINESS	Photography Leisure
ADDRESS	Rochester, N.Y.	EXCHANGE	N.Y.S.E.
TRANSFER AGENT	Lincoln First Bank of Rochester P.O. Box 1250, Rochester, N.Y. 14603	PAR VALUE	$2.50
PARTICIPATING FEATURES		COMMON ~~PREFERRED~~	DATE OF ISSUE
CONVERSION FEATURES		CALLABLE AT	AFTER Y'RS
DIVIDEND DATES	Jan, April, July, Oct.	RATE	YIELD %
WHERE DEPOSITED	Safe Deposit Box	~~MARGINED~~ ~~COLLATERAL~~ OWNED OUTRIGHT	
REMARKS			

	NAME OF BROKER	DATE BOUGHT	No SHARES	CERTIFICATE NUMBER	PRICE PER SHARE	TAX	BROKER COMM.	COST	TOTAL INVESTMENT
A	Bache & Co	6/67	100	RU 117374	70		46.00	7,046 00	7,046 00
B	2/1 Split	5/68	100	RC 125570					7,046 00
C									
D									
E									
F									

	NAME OF BROKER	DATE SOLD	No SHARES	CERTIFICATE NUMBER	PRICE PER SHARE	TAX	BROKER COMM.	AMOUNT REC'D	PROFIT OR LOSS
A									
B									
C									
D									
E									
F									

DIVIDEND RECORD

DATE	RATE	No SHARES	AMOUNT DIVIDEND	DATE	RATE	No SHARES	AMOUNT DIVIDEND	DATE	RATE	No SHARES	AMOUNT DIVIDEND
10/2/67	.40	100	40 00	1/2/70	.53	200	106 00	7/1/72	.26	200	52 00
1/2/68	.90	100	90 00	4/1/70	.25	200	50 00	10/1/72	.26	200	52 00
4/1/68	.40	100	40 00	7/1/70	.25	200	50 00	Total 1972			274 00
7/1/68	.22	200	44 00	10/1/70	.25	200	50 00	1/2/73	.61	200	122 00
10/1/68	.22	200	44 00	Total 1970			256 00	4/2/73	.27	200	54 00
Total 1968			218 00	1/2/71	.57	200	114 00	7/2/73	.27	200	54 00
1/2/69	.50	200	100 00	4/1/71	.25	200	50 00	10/2/73	.45	200	90 00
4/1/69	.22	200	44 00	7/6/71	.25	200	50 00	Total 1973			320 00
7/1/69	.25	200	50 00	10/1/71	.25	200	50 00	1/2/74	.82	200	164 00
10/1/69	.25	200	50 00	Total 1971			264 00	4/1/74	.32	200	64 00
Total 1969			240 00								
				1/3/72	.59	200	118 00				
				4/1/72	.26	200	52 00				

11. Stock Record

can be shown by the Sinclair merger into Atlantic Richfield. This occurred early in 1969 when Atlantic Richfield stock was exchanged for Sinclair stock. Four years later—September 1973 —a lawsuit was scheduled to contest the terms of the merger. *If* you could prove that you owned Sinclair stock between October 1, 1968, and March 4, 1969, you could participate in any benefits arising from the settlement of the lawsuit—even though you may have sold all your stock in the interim. Your old records would provide the necessary proof.

SAFEGUARDING SECURITIES

You can keep your securities safely in one of several ways, depending on your personal preference. The safest procedure is to have the certificates registered in your name and then kept in your safety deposit box at the bank. You alone need have access to it.

If you trade a great deal or travel extensively, you may find it more convenient to establish a *custody account* at your bank. You hold control over buying and selling, and inform the bank of what transactions you make. The bank delivers the securities to your broker or receives them from him for safekeeping. In addition, the bank will make sure the proper dividends and interest are received and will send you a periodic statement. Considering the convenience, safety, and record keeping, the fee your bank charges is very reasonable.

A few brokers provide "safekeeping" service for clients. In this case the securities are registered in your name and address and your broker keeps them in his vault for you. Dividends or interest are paid directly to you by the companies, and the broker sends you a periodic—sometimes a monthly—list of the securities he is keeping for you. The advantages are that you don't have to make a trip to the bank every time you buy or sell and, if you have a bundle of securities, you don't have to rent a larger safety deposit box. The disadvantages are that your securities are not readily available if you need them as collateral for a bank loan, and it might be embarrassing if you decide to change brokers.

The least desirable way to keep securities is in a *street name*. In this case securities are registered either in the name of the brokerage firm or in a fictitious name assigned to your account. Your broker keeps your certificate and sends you a monthly statement showing the securities in your account. It is his duty to credit your account with dividends and interest and he is supposed to forward any company communications to you. For the active trader complete transactions may be made simply by telephone and some record keeping is thus avoided. This method *is not recommended* for the average investor.

INVESTOR PROTECTION

In recent years a number of brokerage firms have merged, dissolved, or gone into bankruptcy. In the process, investors with securities in street names or with cash balances in their account have been either severely inconvenienced or indirectly suffered substantial losses. To protect the small investor, the federal government in 1970 established the Securities Investor Protection Corporation (S.I.P.C.). Simply put, your credit balance with your broker, whether it's cash or securities, is insured in case of bankruptcy in the same manner as the Federal Deposit Insurance Corporation (F.D.I.C.) insures your bank account. The insurance is paid for by the member securities firms and there are limitations on the amount of coverage. This S.I.P.C. has thus made it considerably safer for investors who may have credit balances in their broker accounts.

TRANSFERRING OWNERSHIP

If you sell a security registered in your name, you have to endorse the back of it so that ownership can be transferred. Just as you do not endorse a check until you are ready to cash it, *do not endorse a certificate until you exchange it for a receipt from your broker or banker.* Then keep the receipt until your account has been properly credited.

When you sell a stock and have to mail the certificate to your broker, always send it by *certified mail* and attach a note giving your account number. *Never endorse the certificate.* In a *separate envelope* send him a signed stock or bond power (see Figure 12) and attach a note with your account number. Don't fill in any other spaces except your signature and send this by registered mail also. Your broker will be glad to supply the forms. If either the certificate or the stock power is lost,

IRREVOCABLE STOCK OR BOND POWER

FOR VALUE RECEIVED, the undersigned does (do) hereby sell, assign and transfer to

....

....

.... | ....

(SOCIAL SECURITY OR TAXPAYER IDENTIFYING NO.)

IF STOCK, COMPLETE THIS PORTION

..................shares of the..................stock of..

represented by Certificate(s) No(s)..inclusive,

standing in the name of the undersigned on the books of said Company.

IF BONDS, COMPLETE THIS PORTION

....bonds of..

in the principal amount of $........................., No(s)...................................inclusive,

standing in the name of the undersigned on the books of said Company.

The undersigned does (do) hereby irrevocably constitute and appoint ....

..........................attorney to transfer the said stock or bond(s), as the case may be, on the books of said Company, with full power of substitution in the premises.

Dated.. ....

(PERSON(S) EXECUTING THIS POWER SIGN(S) HERE)

SIGNATURE GUARANTEED

12. Irrevocable Stock or Bond Power

it may cause some inconvenience, but at least you are protected against financial loss.

WHEN A CERTIFICATE IS LOST

In spite of all your precautions, a certificate can be lost. If you do not receive it from your broker after he says it was mailed, it is his responsibility to have it replaced. The same applies in the event of a stock split for which you are to receive an additional certificate. It is the company's responsibility to make sure you get it.

After you have received the certificate, if you discover it has been lost, misplaced, or stolen, *immediately advise the transfer agent* for the company. From your securities record you can give the name of the company, the certificate number, number of shares—common or preferred—and the date of your purchase. You may be required to post a bond to get a replacement certificate, but the transfer agent will explain the proper procedure and your broker will help you with all the communications and forms.

Even though the record- and safekeeping procedures may seem like a lot of work, they are well worth while. Keep up with the job rather than try to catch up. In addition to your own records, you might like to save the annual reports. They can be a source of joy or sometimes of sorrow.

CHAPTER THIRTEEN

The Annual Report

WHAT IT REVEALS AND MAYBE CONCEALS

Corporation officers are as vain as the rest of us and once a year they have the opportunity to brag in print to all the stockholders, competitors, and security analysts about how great they and their companies are. Thus the annual report. As a stockholder, you will receive this report a month or so after the end of the company's accounting year and before the annual stockholders' meeting. Generally speaking, the report covers three broad areas.

DEAR FELLOW STOCKHOLDER

First comes an open letter from the chairman of the board or the president. If business was good during the preceding year the letter is one of self-congratulation and commendations to all the loyal employees. If business was bad—sales and profits declined—then the letter explains all the reasons for this unanticipated turn of events. The only time the letter will come close to blaming management for the poor performance is if the Board of Directors has just recently elected a new president and there has been a general shakeup of top management. Then you will be told how the "new team" plans to do a fine job and overcome the mistakes of the past.

All too often this letter simply takes up space and your time reading it. The *facts* on which to judge management's performance are to be found in the financial section of the report.

WHAT THE COMPANY IS DOING

If like most of us, you don't have the opportunity to keep up to date with a company's day-to-day activities, the second section of the report will interest you. It is a general presentation in words, graphs, and pictures of the major occurrences that have affected the corporation. It will cover such subjects as new products, market areas of operation, or even a natural disaster that has adversely affected operations. It is interestingly prepared to promote what your company is doing and where it is headed.

BEWARE THE CHARTS AND GRAPHS

Although a picture may be worth a thousand words, you have to be extra careful when looking at the charts and graphs that are often included in this section. Too often the *figures are distorted* when someone in the art department turns them into a pretty chart. Two entirely different charts, drawn from the same set of figures, can mislead you. An example is shown in Figure 13.

The top rising line in each graph correctly shows total annual sales. The misleading part is when the chart is also supposed to show you what portion may be foreign and what portion domestic sales. The only difference in the two graphs is that domestic sales are at the bottom and foreign sales at the top in Graph No. 1. They are reversed in Graph No. 2. You can see that the numbers for both are identical, but visually they create different responses. Ignore the graph that purports to show the total make-up of several components.

Multicolored and three-dimensional graphs can create even greater optical illusions, so your safest bet is to *study the figures* from which the graphs are drawn. Admittedly they may be boring, but you won't be deceived by them.

STRAIGHT FACTS

You don't need new math to get information out of the financial section of the annual report. The figures used have

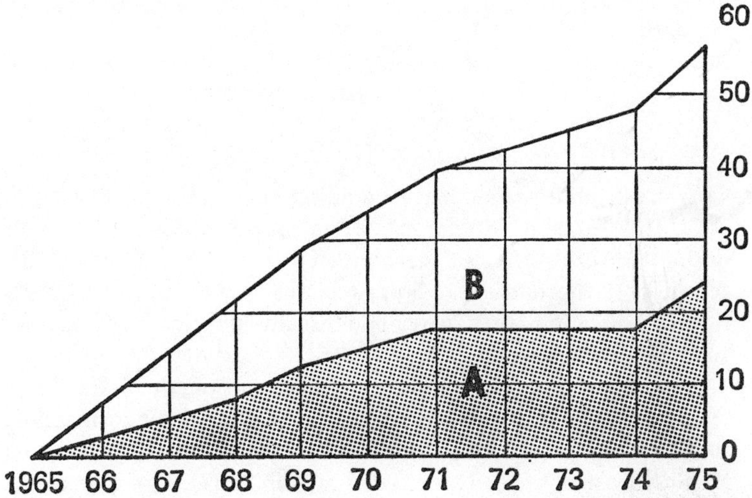

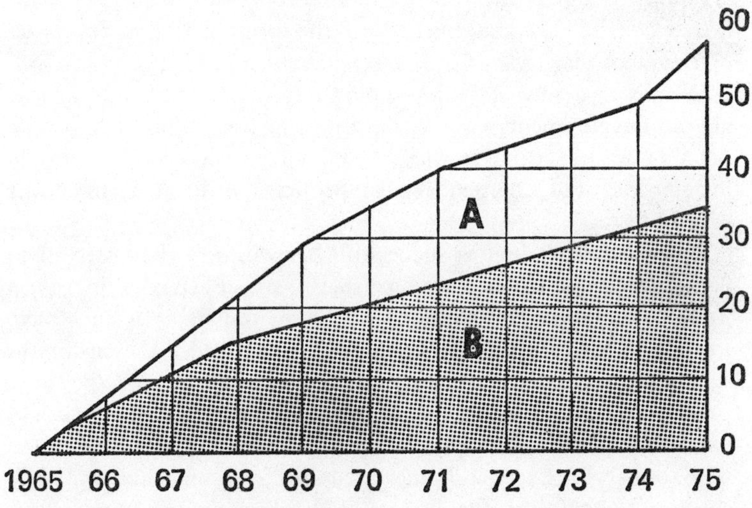

Year	'65	'66	'67	'68	'69	'70	'71	'72	'73	'74	'75
Total Sales (in millions)	0	7.5	15.0	22.5	30.0	35.0	40.0	42.5	45.0	47.5	57.5
A – Export	0	2.5	5.0	7.5	12.5	15.0	17.5	17.5	17.5	17.5	25.0
B – Domestic	0	5.0	10.0	15.0	17.5	20.0	22.5	25.0	27.5	30.0	32.5

13. Sales Graphs

all been taken from the company's bookkeeping records. To insure their accuracy, an outside accounting firm has been hired to review them carefully at the close of the accounting year.

WATCH THE P.S.

You can understand that accounting rules must be flexible in order to be used by companies in many different kinds of business. Also, different accountants interpret the rules differently. If the outside auditors feel that the company's figures need clarification, they may, and usually do, add footnotes to the financial statement.

Sometimes the footnotes are reminiscent of the letter to a friend on vacation; it ended with this P.S.: "I forgot to mention, while telling about our good times here at home, that since you left, your daughter eloped with the milkman, your son was arrested on a narcotics charge, and some way or another your house caught fire and burned to the ground." *The footnotes often reveal more than the financial statement.*

Suppose a company is developing a new product. It can show all the development costs as current expenses. This will reduce profits for the year. Or these costs can be shown as a "capital investment" and charged against profits a little at a time over several years.

If the new product is successful, "expensing" the costs all in one year will *reduce* earnings that year. Then the increased profits from the new product will show up in each successive year. In contrast, if these costs are "capitalized," the profits in successive years will be reduced. Furthermore, if the new product turns out to be a flop after several years of work and expense, the company that "capitalized" the development costs will sooner or later—and unexpectedly for you—have to write them off against profits *in one year.* The company that "expensed" the costs has already subtracted them from profits each year as they were incurred. From the footnotes you can judge for yourself whether the year's profit figure has been overstated or understated.

Then you may see the expression "assuming full dilution." If there are 1,000,000 shares of common stock and the company earns 1,000,000 dollars, the earnings are $1.00 per share. Suppose, however, that there are also convertible bonds and convertible preferred stocks outstanding. If the holders of these securities were to convert them into common stock, then the 1,000,000 dollars of earnings would be *diluted* among more shares of common stock.

Changes in accounting methods from one year to the next, major lawsuits against a company, pending labor negotiations, any restrictive clauses of a bank loan or bond issue, and stock-option plans are among the conditions that may be explained in the footnotes.

Before you review the financial statements, *read the footnotes.* You will then be able to grasp the true meaning of the figures.

HOW DID THIS YEAR COMPARE WITH OTHER YEARS?

Naturally you want to know if your company has annually been increasing sales and profits over *several years.* This information may appear in statistical form in the financial section of the annual report.

If you are primarily investing for income, you will note the dividends per share that have been paid each year. You want not only a continuity of dividends but a *history* of periodic dividend increases to help overcome the rising cost of living.

As for profits or earnings, they are frequently shown as before and also after taxes. The *before tax* figure alerts bondholders because the interest they receive is an expense to the company paid out of earnings before taxes. The *after tax* figure is the one that concerns you as a stockholder. This is the amount that is available, after all expenses have been paid, either to expand the operation of the company or to pay out in dividends.

A *growth company* will hold most, if not all, earnings to reinvest in the business; a company whose stock is recognized as *income* may pay out 60 to 70 per cent of the earnings in dividends. You want to see the total earnings figure increase each year, but check also the *earnings per share* record. If additional stock has been issued, the total earnings figure could have increased with regularity but the earnings for each of your shares may have declined.

This statistical summary offers no assurance of good performance in the future. It does, however, provide an indication of how management has operated the company in the past and might be expected to continue in the future.

WHERE DID IT ALL COME FROM—OR GO TO?

Next look at the *statement of income*. Figures here tell you how the company made its money, how it spent it, and how much money was earned during the year covered by the report. Ordinarily, figures are shown for both the current and the preceding year, thus giving you an idea of whether or not there has been improvement.

If you own bonds, you want to know that enough money has been earned to pay you the interest. A safe rule of thumb is for the *operating profit—total income*, minus day-to-day expenses—to equal three or four times the total of the interest the company has had to pay. Thus, if a company shows an operating profit of $100,000 and the total annual interest is $25,000, you are assured of receiving your interest as it comes due. Keep in mind that interest is a tax-deductible expense for a company; the profit figure that concerns you is *before taxes*.

As a *preferred stockholder* you care about the safety of your dividend. The preferred dividend, like the common stock dividend, is not tax deductible for the company and is paid out of profits; so look at *net earnings after taxes*. If this figure is ten times the preferred dividends, you can be fairly sure of receiving dividends regularly on your preferred stock.

After *all expenses and preferred dividends* have been paid, what is left is available to the common stockholders. You want to see the *earnings per share*—that is, the total remaining income divided by the total number of common shares—increase from last year. It is the company management who determine how much to pay out in dividends, how much to retain for future expansion.

WHERE DOES THIS LEAVE THE COMPANY?

Now that the income statement has shown you what the company did during the year, the next question is, Where does it leave the company at the end of the year? The *balance sheet* shows what the company owns and what is owed to it by others —*assets*. It also shows what the company owes to others—*liabilities*.

If all the assets were turned into cash to pay all liabilities, whatever is left over would belong to the stockholders and is known variously as stockholders' equity or net worth of the company. It is then obvious that the sum of the liabilities and the net worth always add up to whatever the assets may be.

Assets and liabilities are of two kinds—current and long-term. *Current assets* include everything that will be converted into cash in the normal course of business, as inventory. Buildings, machinery, and such are the long-term assets the company expects to keep. Similarly, *current liabilities* include debts due to be paid *within one year*. Long-term liabilities are debts not due for possibly several years—bank loans or bonds.

WHAT TO LOOK FOR

You want to see that the total assets are greater than the total liabilities. If they aren't, there is no stockholder equity and the company is broke.

The amount of money the company has available to use, *working capital*, is the difference between current assets and current liabilities. The amount needed varies with the type and size of a business. The Fuller Brush man needs very little working capital because he has few expenses and no inventory to pay for until after a customer buys. A specialty shop, on the other hand, must have greater working capital with which to pay rent, utilities, clerks' salaries and to buy inventory.

HOW MUCH IS ENOUGH WORKING CAPITAL?

How much working capital is enough can be discovered by comparing one company with another in the same line of business. Although size is a factor, you don't have to find the same size company for comparison. If you *divide current assets by current liabilities you can get the current ratio*. If one company has current assets of $3 million and current liabilities of $1.5 million, the current ratio is two to one. A much larger company in the same industry with current assets of $40 million and current liabilities of $20 million would also have a current ratio of two to one. If the company you are considering has a current ratio far different from others in the same industry, beware. Too high a ratio may mean management is not using assets to best advantage; too low a ratio could indicate severe financial straits.

A current ratio of two to one is generally considered acceptable.

The glossy cover of your annual report, the glowing prose, the colorful pictures and graphs are aimed at convincing you that *your* management and *your* company are top quality. Too often a report shows that an inordinate amount of management's time and your money have been spent on this sales effort. The S.E.C. is trying to overcome this by encouraging greater factual reporting. Until this happens, look to the financial section in the annual report for the *facts* on which to evaluate your investment.

CHAPTER FOURTEEN

The Quarterly Checkup

YOUR OWN PORTFOLIO MANAGEMENT

Just as a company makes a regular report on its progress, you will do well to make up a quarterly report on your own investment progress. In order to do this you have to know how to get the current facts about your stocks.

It has been pointed out that when you buy and sell stocks your broker gives you current quotations, but you shouldn't bombard him with requests for quotations needlessly. In between transactions with him, get the current prices from the financial pages of your newspaper. They will be adequate for your needs as an average investor—not a speculative trader. The New York and the American Stock Exchange Quotations are similar in format and easy to understand. Here is a sample.

READING MARKET QUOTATIONS

The first two figures before the company name indicate the highest and lowest prices paid in the current year. If the stock is traded at a new high or a new low, these figures are changed.

You will also see a change at the beginning of March. Since these figures are intended to show a trading range—highest and lowest—over a period of time, the previous year's prices are included through the first two months or so of the next year. Thus in February the highest and lowest prices may be 62 and 43. Later, in March, when last year's prices are discarded and only the current year's highs and lows are shown, the figures may be 58 and 54. These prices are important to you. A comparison with

1975 High	Low	Stocks and Div. In Dollars	P/E	Sales 100s	High	Low	Last	Net Chg
24¾	20½	Borden 1.30	8	363	23¼	22½	22¾	+ ⅛
17⅜	13⅛	BorWar 1.35	6	83	17¼	16¾	17⅛	......
2⅞	1¼	Bormans	7	14	2¾	2⅝	2¾	+ ⅛
20⅜	15½	BosEd 2.44	7	95	19½	19	19	— ⅛
90	70	BosE pf8.88	...	z10	86	86	86	......
8¾	5	Braniff .20e	6	500	8½	8⅛	8⅜	......
43½	36½	BriggS 1.60a	12	42	39⅝	38¾	38⅞	— 1⅛
63¼	46½	BristMy 1.60	17	128	62⅝	62	62⅛	......
39⅜	33	BristM pf 2	...	14	39½	39¼	39½	+ ⅛
10⅜	4½	BritPet .40e	2	388	9⅜	9⅛	9¼	— ½
16	12¾	Brkwy Gls .1	6	83	16	15⅝	16	+ ⅛
17	11⅞	BklyUG 1.72	7	17	16⅜	16⅛	16⅛	— ⅜
11⅜	9½	Brown Co	2	5	10¾	10⅜	10¾	+ ⅛
17¾	13½	BwnGp 1.60	9	110	18¾	17	18¾	+ 2¼
7¼	4⅞	BwnShrp .20	5	19	6¾	6½	6¾	— ⅛
8¼	5	BrwnFer .20	8	150	7¼	7	7¼	+ ¼
12⅜	9	Brunswk .40	6	564	12¾	12⅛	12¾	+ ⅝
12	9¼	BrushW .40	4	9	11¾	11⅝	11¾	+ ⅛
6	3½	BT Mt 1.15e	...	72	4⅝	4	4⅝	+ ½
38½	31¾	BucyErie 1	15	48	33¾	33⅛	33½	— ½
10⅛	7⅛	BuddCo .80	6	92	10	9¾	9⅞	......
5	4½	BudCa pf.60	...	3	5	5	5	......
3½	2¾	BudtInd .22t	4	5	3¼	3⅛	3⅛	— ⅛
17	12	BuffFor 1.20	16	x11	17	16½	16½	— ⅛
8½	7	BulovaW .70	6	20	8½	8½	8½	......
22⅛	19¾	BunkHil 1.92	...	13	21⅛	21	21	— ½
6¼	3¼	BunkrRa .40	9	131	7	6¼	7	+ ¾
13⅞	9⅞	Bunkr pf1.60	...	10	14	13⅝	13⅝	— ⅛
21¾	14⅞	Burllnd 1.20	7	326	21½	20¾	21⅜	+ ⅜

14. Stock Quotations

the current price gives an indication of whether the price is moving higher, lower, or staying just about the same as earlier in the year.

After the name of the company the amount of the annual dividend per share will be given. Some quotations include a column with the current per cent yield. If yours doesn't, figure it out by dividing the current stock price, say 50, into the amount of the dividend, say 2. Thus the yield is .04 or 4 per cent.

The figures used in computing the price/earnings ratio are the last traded price divided by the last twelve months' earnings as reported by the company—*not* the amount earned in the last calendar year. Let's say the company announces that between September of last year and September of this year earnings per share were $1.40. If the stock is selling for 11¼, the P/E ratio is eight—$11.25÷$1.40. The ratio figure changes as either price or earnings change.

The Sales-in-100s column tells you how many shares were traded the previous day. Thus, if the figure 17 appears, 1,700 shares were traded, but this does not include the number traded as odd lots—that is, less than a hundred shares. Watching this volume of shares traded over a period of time, you get a pretty good idea of how active the stock is. If the stock hasn't been traded at all, the company will not even appear on the list.

The next three columns show the highest, lowest, and last trading prices for the day. In the case of weekly quotations, as in Barron's or in most Sunday newspapers, they are the aggregate. Prices are quoted in dollars and eighths of a dollar thus:

⅛=12½¢	⅝=62½¢
¼=25¢	¾=75¢
⅜=37½¢	⅞=87½¢
½=50¢	

The Net Change figures show the price difference between the closing prices of two successive days—or weeks, in the case of weekly quotations. It's natural to be favorably impressed when you see a net change of plus 5, but sometimes a plus ⅛ is actually a higher gain. For example, if a stock closed at 300 yesterday and closes at 305 today, the gain is 1.66 per cent. If a $5.00 stock goes up ⅛ to $5.125, it is a 2.5 per cent gain. Three hundred dollars invested in each would end up as $305 and $307.50 respectively. When you are reading market quotations or talking with other investors, remind yourself that *the per cent change, not the dollar change, is the important factor.*

HOW DID YOURS PERFORM?

Just as TV commercials urge you to compare results of one product with another, you should also compare your investment results from time to time with some investment standard. You can use one of the various market indexes as your standard, but *select one that is similar to your own portfolio.*

If your portfolio consists of common stocks of top-quality industrial companies, you might use Standard & Poor's 425 Industrial Stock Price Index or the Dow Jones (30 stock) Industrial Average. These two are widely used barometers of *industrial stock* prices; they provide a relatively good indication of the way the market is moving.

Your portfolio may include airline or utility stocks in addition to industrial stocks. In that case you want to compare your portfolio with a standard that includes stocks in these industries. The Dow Jones 65 Stock Average and the Standard & Poor's 500 Stock Average would then be more representative for your purpose.

Although these indexes have been around for some years, many portfolio managers feel that they are based on too small a group of too select securities and therefore aren't representative of the *entire* market. For comparison purposes, they rely on the New York Stock Exchange Index, the American Stock Exchange Index, or the National Association of Securities Dealers' Index (N.A.S.D.A.Q.) of over-the-counter securities. If your portfolio consists of securities that are not generally classified as blue-chip or industry leaders, you might do well to follow these other indexes.

Investment performance is relative. If the market is generally going up, as from 1962 through 1965, or is generally going down, as from 1969 through mid-1970, your stock performance must be measured against these changing conditions. Don't judge simply whether your portfolio is worth more or worth less than when you started. But if market values generally went up 20 per cent and your portfolio went up only 10 per cent, you did not do too well, even though the dollar value of your portfolio was greater.

Your first step is to make a record of the total value of your portfolio and the index that you have selected as a standard. Regularly thereafter, perhaps every three months, figure the total value of your investments and divide the amount by the starting value. Your answer will be the current value of your portfolio expressed as a *per cent of the original value.*

Thus, if you had investments worth $45,000 at the outset and three months later they are worth $48,000, your arithmetic will give you an answer of 1.066—or an increase of 6.6 per cent. If during the same period your standard, let's say the N.Y.S.E. Index, rose from 59.44 to 61.88, dividing the current value by the starting value will give you an answer of 1.040—or an increase of 4 per cent.

Even when both your portfolio and the index are declining, the answer from dividing the portfolio values should be higher than from dividing the index values. If the portfolio dropped from $45,000 to $43,650 and the standard from 57.06 to 54.77, your arithmetic answers will be 97 and 96 per cent respectively. In other words, your portfolio declined only 3 per cent while the standard dropped 4 per cent.

Any time your arithmetic gives a higher answer for the standard market index than for your portfolio, start searching for trouble areas and the stocks that are causing your *relatively* poor performance.

PRELIMINARY PORTFOLIO ANALYSIS

It's one thing to complain about the high cost of groceries and quite another to lower your expenditures. To do this, you have to examine the many items you buy and determine which may be unnecessary and which brands are too high priced. In the same way, periodically check your portfolio and decide whether each investment is the best buy *for your purposes.* Then you will be in a strong position to discuss recommendations with your broker or adviser.

First separate your investments *by industry* and figure the current market value of each. Right away you can see whether the bulk of your portfolio is invested in a single industry. This is

PRELIMINARY PORTFOLIO ANALYSIS

	Nov. Market Value	Per Cent of Portfolio
AEROSPACE:		
100 United Aircraft	2,837.50	18.9
AUTOMOTIVE:		
50 Ford Motor Co.	1,593.75	10.7
INSURANCE:		
50 Aetna Life Ins.	1,150.00	7.7
OILS:		
50 Exxon	3,443.75	23.0
STEELS:		
100 Bethlehem Steel	2,812.50	18.8
UTILITIES:		
100 Public Service of Indiana	3,112.50	20.8
TOTAL PORTFOLIO	14,950.00	100.0
Dow Jones Ind. Avg.	665.52	
N.Y.S.E. Index	38.97	

15. Preliminary Portfolio Analysis

great as long as that industry is performing well, like the hotel-motel business from mid-1970 through 1971. But in 1972 the bottom dropped out and all gains were lost. The conservative approach is to spread your risk among different industries. You might not make as much but you are not likely to lose as much either if you have spread your portfolio among four or more industries with not more than 25 per cent in any one.

Figure 15 shows a sample analysis, the percentage figures obtained by dividing the total portfolio value into the market value of each industry. It is immediately apparent that no one industry dominates these investments. If any of your percentage figures amount to more than 25 per cent *for one industry*, you would do well to start looking for diversification. Your search would immediately eliminate all other companies in the same industry. *Always keep your investment objective in mind when you are looking for another stock to buy.*

PERIODIC REVIEW

Once you have made the desired changes, you can set up a more elaborate analysis for periodic portfolio review. The sample shown in Figure 16 may be more detailed than you need and certain columns can be eliminated. If you aren't too concerned with capital gains taxes, the cost figures may be eliminated. If you aren't too interested in income, then leave out the yield and annual income columns. And if you are not investing for growth, there is no need to compute the percentage change of each stock, although you will want to keep an eye on whether any particular investment is losing money.

The sample shown can be used to analyze any size portfolio with any objective; it provides *facts* on which to base your investment decisions. Because the facts are constantly changing, it is up to you to keep your analysis up to date every three months or so.

There are powerful arguments in favor of this work, for it is *your money* you are supervising. Furthermore, it dampens any tendency to trade excessively without good cause. Finally, you have greater *confidence* if you *know* what your investments are doing.

16. Periodic Portfolio Review

PERIODIC PORTFOLIO REVIEW

NAME AND QUANTITY	Total Cost	10/31/74 Market Value	2/28/75 Market Value	Quarterly % Change	Current Per Cent Yield	Indicated Annual Income	Per Cent of Portfolio
AEROSPACE:							
100 United Aircraft	2,150.00	2,837.50	3,600.00	26.87	5.55	200.00	21.76
AUTOMOTIVE:							
50 Ford Motor Co.	2,287.50	1,593.75	1,650.00	3.53	9.69	160.00	9.97
INSURANCE:							
50 Aetna Life Ins.	2,262.50	1,150.00	1,112.50	–3.26	4.85	54.00	6.73
OILS:							
50 Exxon	2,862.50	3,443.75	3,868.75	12.34	6.66	257.50	23.38
STEELS:							
100 Bethlehem Steel	2,850.00	2,812.50	2,962.50	5.33	9.28	275.00	17.91
UTILITIES:							
100 Public Service Ind.	2,800.00	3,112.50	3,350.00	7.63	7.64	256.00	20.25
TOTAL PORTFOLIO	15,212.50	14,950.00	16,543.75	10.66	7.27	1,202.50	100.00
Dow Jones Ind. Avg.		665.52	739.05	11.05			
N.Y.S.E. Index		38.97	43.07	10.52			

PART FOUR

When You Have Gained Experience

CHAPTER FIFTEEN

New Issues and Secondary Offerings

SHOULD THEY TEMPT YOU?

New issues and secondary offerings require the services of an *underwriter*, who arranges the *orderly sale* of a large quantity of securities. An underwriter may be an investment banker or a broker who has sufficient resources to buy large amounts of stocks or bonds from a seller in a single transaction. The securities may be those of a company just being formed and looking for financing through sales of stock to the public, or those of an established company looking for new financing. In some cases the seller may be a *major* stockholder. Regardless of who the seller is or for what purpose the securities are being sold, the objective is for the owner to receive a fair value for his securities.

THE UNDERWRITER AND HIS JOB

The underwriter agrees to buy all the securities *for a specific price*. It is not his intention to own them for any length of time. On that account he must have an organization capable of selling the securities in smaller quantities to other investors. If the value of the securities is exceptionally large, the underwriter may enlist the aid of other brokers to form a *selling group*, or two or more firms may join and form an *underwriting syndicate* to buy the securities.

The underwriter assures the seller of the securities of immediate payment of a specific sum of money. In return for this prompt payment and for the effort required to resell the securities, the underwriter receives a negotiated fee from the seller. This fee takes the place of the broker's normal commission.

NEW ISSUES

Don't fall into the habit of many small investors who think of new issues only in terms of common stocks. New issues are also composed of preferred stocks and bonds. These may range from ultra conservative to highly speculative. In any case a new issue is a security that has *never before been registered* with the Securities and Exchange Commission for sale to the general public. If your broker or adviser suggests a new issue, he is required to give you a prospectus on the offering. (See Chapter Sixteen, "The Prospectus.") Read this carefully word for word and cover to cover. The prospectus contains essential information.

When your broker calls you about a new issue he will doubtless offer the enticement that "there is no commission involved." Technically he is right, but you know he isn't selling stock just for the fun of it. When you read the prospectus, you will see that the underwriter's fee may be considerably more than a broker's fee for a stock of equivalent price that was already being traded.

As an example, take a new issue priced at $16.50 per share. The prospectus tells you the *proceeds to the seller*—that is, the value of the security—will be $15.10; the *underwriting* discount or payment will be $1.40—a sum equal to 9¼ per cent of the proceeds. At current commission rates on 100 shares of stock now trading at $15 on a stock exchange, the commission would be $34.65 or 2.3 per cent. In each case you are buying a $15 stock. Granted, for the underwriter there is a great deal more risk and effort involved in a new issue, but for you there is no value added to the stock.

"There is no commission to you" is probably the most often used sales pitch for a new issue, and a most alluring phrase it is to a good many investors. But it is the least valid reason for buying a new issue or any other investment.

THE GOOD AND THE BAD

As pointed out, new issues are securities never before offered to the public. Under this broad classification you will find many good values. A well-established, profitable company may find it advisable to raise additional cash by selling a new issue of preferred stocks or bonds. The money may be earmarked for expansion or to pay off high-interest loans and create greater profit. New issues of this type should be considered by the conservative investor because there is already a history of performance on which to base an investment decision. If the existing stocks or bonds of the company represent a good investment the new issue might be even more attractive.

Bull markets offer the best opportunity not only for good companies but also for "leaky roof" operations to find investors. In a roaring bull market a multitude of new issues come on the market. If investor psychology is ripe, brokers may even ration these securities, preference going to their largest and best customers. In this climate an aura of respectability and desirability is imparted to even the most speculative issues. Too often it is this aura that drives the market price to ridiculous levels. When the aura fades the price is all too likely to plummet, as was the case with the disastrous National Student Marketing stock.

As a careful investor, you should follow one of two procedures: Don't buy new issues of little-known or inexperienced companies or, if you do, sell at the end of a week or two *regardless of whether or not you show a profit.* If you have a profit, be satisfied even though the price may continue to rise. If you have a loss, don't compound the error by hanging on with the eternal hope that the price will recover.

Studies made of times when new issues have appeared at a rapid rate show that several years later many of the companies had disappeared and only a fraction of the survivors was operating at a profit. Obviously you are better off considering speculative new issues as short-term investments, if at all. The odds against finding a budding Xerox or IBM are tremendous—a professional gambler would never take such a chance. You will be wise to leave new issues to the high-risk-oriented investor.

SECONDARY OFFERINGS

If you have ever been approached for a new issue, then you have no doubt been solicited for a secondary offering. The two are similar and the "no commission" sales pitch is applicable to both. The secondary offering is necessary when a large block of stock—relative to the quantities normally traded—is to be offered. If this large block were to be sold in the normal way it would create a glut on the market and the price would be abnormally depressed. Not only would the seller receive less than a fair price for his shares, but other owners of the stock would suffer a loss on their investment. Even though the stock has already been registered with the Securities and Exchange Commission and shares are being regularly traded, a prospectus is made available with the most current information and an underwriter engaged.

The price of the stock is ordinarily a fraction less than the closing market price the day before the secondary offering is available to the public. This lower price together with no commission provides an incentive to buy, and helps the underwriter sell the total amount of stock offered. As with new issues, however, don't let this be the sole basis for your investment.

When you hear of a secondary offering by one or two large stockholders, it's logical to wonder whether they have some inside information that will cause the price to drop when what they know becomes known to the public. Trading on inside information is illegal and the penalties can more than wipe out any profits that have been made.

The fact is that the sellers of the stock usually consider the money can be better invested elsewhere *for their particular objectives*. The successful company founder may decide to sell a large part of his ownership as an aspect of his estate planning. Or he may feel that if more shares were in the hands of the public, a wider market would be created for the remainder of his shares that will be sold at a later date. A large-growth-oriented investor may feel that he has realized his objective with this particular stock and decide to take his profit and invest elsewhere. It is difficult to ascribe reasons for secondary offerings, but they are prompted more often by legitimate business reasons than by subterfuge.

AFTER THE UNDERWRITING

New issues and secondary offerings are promoted with a good deal of advance publicity, and underwriters invest a great deal of money, time, and effort in the sale of all the shares being offered. If the underwriting of a secondary offering is successful and the shares are all sold, normal trading in the stock has been affected very little. If a new issue has been successfully sold the new stock will start being traded just like any other stock.

On the other hand, an offering may be very poorly received by investors, and after a reasonable length of time the underwriters may find themselves stuck with a lot of unsold shares. At this point the underwriting syndicate is dissolved and the remaining shares are sold for whatever investors will pay for them. This might be quite a bit less than the offering price. The underwriters, having promised the sellers a specific price, will lose money and the investors who bought the stock under the terms of the offering will also see their investment drop in value.

The guidelines for investing in new issues and secondary offerings are the same as for the rest of your portfolio. Learn all you can about the offerings first. Base your decision on facts. *The absence of a commission is an incentive and not a reason to invest.*

CHAPTER SIXTEEN

The Prospectus

TRUTH AND DREAM

RECIPE FOR DISILLUSIONMENT

Take any economy expanding too rapidly, add:

An overabundance of new issues and secondary offerings
Exuberant brokers making commissions on the underwritings
An inflationary fueled stock market
A new crop of novice investors dreaming of overnight wealth

Mix together in ever increasing proportions over a period of many months until the whole batch disintegrates into little pieces.

Nineteen-seventy might be called a year of disillusionment. Market averages tumbled. Brokerage firms fought for survival—a fight that quite a few lost. Brokers who had been making huge commissions up to the end of the sixties left the business for more secure employment. Investors were vowing never again to be roped in. It was not a novel situation because the recipe has been tried many times, and with the same results. It was most successful in 1929 and 1930, and led Congress to pass several acts to help protect investors. Not the least of these was the *Securities Act of 1933*, which was a mild form of consumer protection. In a nutshell, the act requires *full disclosure* of all relevant facts about a corporation before its securities may be offered to the public. It's unfortunate that so few investors take advantage of this full disclosure and consequently find themselves stuck with an investment of far less value than they expected.

WHAT IS A PROSPECTUS?

This full disclosure by a corporation is made in a lengthy two-part *registration statement.* This is filed with the Securities and Exchange Commission. The first part is the *prospectus.* Whenever you are solicited for a new issue or a secondary offering, ask for a copy. In it you will find all the favorable facts that your broker has already given you. More important, you will discover facts that you may consider negative, and these may be far more relevant to the value of the investment.

You can get a prospectus on any company whose securities are available for trading by the public. However, if the company has not recently offered any new common or preferred stocks, bonds, or warrants (see Chapter Seventeen, "Rights and Warrants") the information may be somewhat out of date. The prospectus, therefore, is most useful and up to date in evaluating securities in the process of being offered to the public for the first time.

On the cover of the prospectus you will find routine information—the name of the corporation, the number and type of securities offered, and whether they are being sold directly by the company or by other large investors, such as the founders of the company. You will also see exactly how much you, the public, must pay for the securities, how much will go to the sellers of the securities, and how much will be paid to the underwriters in commissions or discounts. The price to the public might be $35, out of which $2.00 goes to the underwriters as discounts and commissions and $33 goes to the company or selling stockholders. This gives the lie to the sales pitch that "you don't have to pay a commission." It would be more accurate for a broker to tell you that the commission is included in the stock price and is not charged later.

In 1967 and '68 many small investors bought new issues that subsequently plummeted in value, and they vowed never to buy stocks again. Possibly their brokers did not warn them that the stock was a gamble. Had they read the prospectus they would have noted a *front-page* warning to the effect that the securities offered should be regarded as highly speculative. To this day these investors blame their brokers and the stock market in general, but really it was their own fault. They did not heed the *full disclosure* that was available to them.

INVESTOR, PROTECT THYSELF!

In the hope that the investor will try to protect himself or herself from being misled, an admonition appears on the inside page of the prospectus: "No person has been authorized to give any information or make any representation not contained in this prospectus and, if given or made, such information or representation must not be relied upon as having been authorized." That strikes me as a pretty strong warning to an investor to examine the facts and not rely entirely on the sales pitch of an exuberant salesman. Yet there are many investors who prefer to act on a glowing report from a salesman—who is bound to be prejudiced—than investigate for themselves. I fear they deserve the losses they experience.

RELEVANT INFORMATION

In addition to the names of the directors and major stockholders, detailed financial information, and a general description of the business, you will find many other relevant facts in the prospectus. These have varying degrees of influence on the value of an investment, and you may evaluate them differently from someone trying to sell you the stock. It's like spilling wine on your dress—you are upset over the stain, another points out the loss of the wine, and a third regards the accident as unimportant.

Your broker may consider it immaterial that just a few persons own the majority of the stock and control the company; consequently he may not point this out. You should consider whether you wouldn't prefer an investment in which control is spread among a great many stockholders. The prospectus will give you this necessary information about a company.

A pending lawsuit or labor unrest is not an encouraging feature of a stock so the salesman soliciting your investment may neglect to mention it. Under the rules of full disclosure, these facts are brought out and available to anyone interested in reading about them. Information about management, products, and competition is also revealed.

It is these facts that are the basis on which you should make your investment decision. If you have doubts about any of them, go to your broker with *specific knowledgeable questions*—and get answers. Then you will never be in the embarrassing position of claiming that "nobody told me this about the company."

AFTER YOU INVEST

Long after you have made your decision whether or not to invest, the knowledge you have gained from the prospectus will be important to you as an investor. Subsequent news articles will be relevant because you will be able to relate them to your decision.

Examining a 1972 prospectus for Waste Management, Inc., I noticed a section entitled "Certain Factors to Be Considered." Five specific parts of the prospectus were cited as being particularly important and were singled out as cautions to the investor. Among them was "regulation by federal, state, and local authorities." Reading on, I discovered that the "regulation" referred to such matters as water, air, and noise pollution; fire prevention; pest control; zoning and land-use restrictions. Whenever you learn of a new regulation in these areas, you can immediately consider the impact on your investment and then make a reasonable decision whether to buy or sell.

The information you get from the prospectus doesn't guarantee a profitable investment decision, but it will help you invest intelligently instead of blindly following someone's advice and simply hoping for the best.

℞ FOR DISILLUSIONMENT

Read the prospectus for *full disclosure* about any investment you are considering.

CHAPTER SEVENTEEN

Rights and Warrants

MORE OPPORTUNITIES

Rights and warrants are both forms of an agreement between an issuing company and the holder. The agreement entitles the holder to buy stock in the company at a specified price over a specified period of time with no broker's commission. Until the time period elapses, rights and warrants may be bought or sold. *Upon expiration of the specified time period, they have no value.*

The difference between the two is principally the time period. Rights may give a holder an investment opportunity for only a month or two. Warrants may not expire for several years. In some cases they are perpetual and never expire.

Rights

You may own stock in a company that has issued one million shares but is authorized under its bylaws to issue a total of two million shares. If more working capital is needed the company may decide to sell an additional half million shares of stock. The company could employ an underwriter to sell the stock to other investors. (See Chapter Fifteen, "New Issues and Secondary Offerings.") The drawback to this is that the *existing stockholders,* instead of owning 100 per cent of the *issued* stock, would end up owning one million shares out of a total of one and a half million shares of the *issued* stock—only 66⅔ per cent of the total. Their ownership would be reduced by one third. There is also the cost to the company of attracting these new investors.

The solution for the company is to issue rights to the *current stockholders.*

In this case, you would be issued one right for each share you own, and the company would issue a total of one million rights. Since there are only five hundred thousand shares to be sold, the company would specify that two rights would be required to buy one of the new shares.

The price of the stock, as specified in the right, is normally slightly lower than the closing market price on the day before the rights are issued. The slightly *lower price*, together with *no broker's commission*, provides an *incentive* for the existing stockholders to increase their stock ownership.

Let's say the stock is selling at $20 and two rights are required to buy one share at $19—the *exercise price*. This makes the two rights worth $1.00 or 50 cents each. If the stock should go to $21, your rights would still entitle you to buy at $19; so your two rights would now be worth $2.00, or $1.00 each. As you can see in this example, the value of your right is the difference between the exercise price, which is fixed, and the market price, which varies.

Consider also that, when you exercise your right and buy at $19, there is no commission. This feature gives your right a token value even though the market price may drop to $19—the same level as the exercise price.

PRE-EMPTIVE RIGHTS

To avoid confusion, it may be a good idea to explain here *pre-emptive rights*. The bylaws of some companies stipulate that no new common or preferred stock—share ownership in the company—may be sold to the public without first offering it to the current stockholders. This stipulation is known as pre-emptive rights.

In our example of a company wanting to sell five hundred thousand additional shares, pre-emptive rights in the bylaws would require the company to make a rights offering to the existing stockholders. Without pre-emptive rights, the company would be free to sell the five hundred thousand shares to whomever it chose, and the existing stockholders' percentage ownership would be reduced.

WHAT TO DO WITH YOUR RIGHTS

When your company issues rights you are notified and receive a lengthly but simple form to fill out and return. You have three choices:

1. You can sell the rights. Complete the appropriate part of the form and return it to the company along with the rights. When the offering expires, you will receive a check from the company for whatever price the company was able to get for your rights. If you originally owned one hundred shares out of one million and sold your rights, you would then own only one hundred shares out of one and a half million. Your percentage ownership thus would be reduced.

2. You can buy more shares. If you have an *exact* number of rights to buy shares, complete the appropriate form. Return this to the company together with the rights and your check for the number of shares you are buying multiplied by the exercise price. In our example your one hundred shares would entitle you to one hundred rights. Since the terms of the offering require two rights to buy one share at $19, you would be entitled to buy fifty shares. Your check would be for $950–50×$19. At the conclusion of the rights offering you would receive your stock certificate for the additional shares.

3. You can juggle the rights offering to suit your pocketbook. If you don't have the $950 to buy fifty shares and have only $475 in the bank, you can buy twenty-five shares and sell the balance of your rights. In this case you would use fifty rights to make the purchase and instruct the company to sell the remaining fifty rights to another investor.

The reverse of this situation would be if you had $1,200 in the bank and wanted to invest it all in the company. At $19 per share, you could afford to buy sixty shares; so you buy fifty with the one hundred rights you own and instruct the company to buy an additional twenty rights–from a selling rights holder–and use these to buy the additional ten shares you want. Of course, if there are no sellers of the rights, the company can't comply with your instructions and the money you sent for the extra ten shares would be returned.

At the conclusion of the offering the company settles up with everyone who returned rights. You would receive a check if you sold the rights, a stock certificate if you bought stock, and a bill if you bought additional rights. Regardless of your choice, *don't simply let rights expire*—they do have value.

Warrants

Warrants are similar to rights to the extent that they give the holder the privilege of buying stock at a specified price. The life of a warrant is measured in years compared to weeks for rights. Because of this warrants have many of the investment features of common stock but warrants are issued for a different reason.

WHY WARRANTS ARE ISSUED

At a time of investor indifference a company may have to raise additional cash and decide to sell a new issue of securities —stocks or bonds. Management may conclude that the fair price for the securities will not arouse enough investor interest to insure raising all the required money. Just as a breakfast-cereal manufacturer may enclose a coupon good toward your next purchase, management may decide to include a warrant with the securities offer at no extra cost. The primary purpose in both instances is to make the initial purchase more attractive. The secondary purpose is to set the stage for a repeat sale. At some time before the expiration of the warrant, it is hoped, the holder will exercise the privilege of buying the stock at the specified price. Until the expiration date the warrants are traded just like stocks.

HOW VALUABLE ARE WARRANTS?

If a warrant entitles you to buy a share of stock at $50 and the stock is currently trading at $60, it is apparent that the warrant is worth $10. As the price of the stock goes up or down, the warrant value rises and falls an equal amount. The value is somewhat altered because, if the stock and warrant prices rise or fall $1.00, you gain or lose less than 2 per cent on your *stock* investment compared to 10 per cent on your *warrant* investment. You might expect to pay a slight premium for the warrant because of this speculative leverage. On the other hand, as a warrant holder, you do not receive any dividends and this tends to lessen the premium. The warrant value in this example, therefore, merely approximates the difference between the exercise price and the stock price.

Suppose the market price of this same stock drops to $40, which is $10 *less* than the exercise price. The warrants still have value even though it may be minimal, because there are investors around who are willing to take the risk that the stock price will rise above the exercise price. Of course, as the market price of the stock declines, so does the warrant price. The lower the stock price goes, the more speculative the warrants become.

ARE WARRANTS SPECULATIVE?

Let's assume you have $1,500 to invest. You can buy twenty-five shares of stock trading at $60 or you can buy 150 warrants for the same stock at $10 for the same total amount of money. If the stock price rises $5.00, your twenty-five shares will be worth $1,625. The warrants will also have increased $5.00 each and your hundred and fifty warrants will now be worth $2,250. This sounds great, but the same principle applies when the stock and warrants go down in price. A $5.00 drop in value creates a $125 loss on the stock investment and a $750 loss on the warrant investment. In this case the warrants are a more speculative investment than the stock.

On the other hand, warrants can be very conservative. Given the same $1,500 and assuming all you would ever want to own is twenty-five shares of the stock, you could buy twenty-five warrants for $250 and put the remaining $1,250 in a savings bank. No matter how high the price of the stock goes, you can exercise your warrants to buy the stock with your savings balance. Conversely, if the stock drops to zero, the maximum loss you will have on your warrants is $250 and your $1,250 will be safe.

The degree of speculation depends therefore on the amount of your investment funds you use to buy warrants.

WHO SHOULD BUY WARRANTS?

In the late 1960s there was a rash of new issues in untried and unproven companies. It is tempting for even conservative investors to buy some of these speculative stocks. If you get the urge to speculate, buy warrants issued by *known* companies, rather than new stock issued by *unknown* companies. The known companies stand a better chance of being around a few years hence.

You may find yourself with limited cash to invest in a stock that you are convinced is going up. If warrants are available, you may be able to afford a hundred warrants for a lower commission than on the odd-lot number of shares.

There are those who would prefer to give a child a hundred A.T.&T. warrants rather than ten shares of A.T.&T. stock for roughly the same cost. The logic is that the child has no income requirement and the warrant has a much better chance than the stock of doubling in value. It comes back to the degree of speculation you can afford.

If you can't afford to speculate at all, avoid warrants.

CHAPTER EIGHTEEN

Options—Puts and Calls

FOR THE EXPERIENCED INVESTOR

As an experienced investor with money to spare, you may care to get involved in options. Option trading is more complicated than ordinary stock trading. If you are willing to trade a fair amount you can use options to good conservative advantage or for outright speculation. In the same way that you can conceivably find another investor on your own with whom to trade stock, so too you could possibly find another investor to trade options. As with stocks and bonds, your broker provides the most efficient procedure.

Since the recent start of option trading on some exchanges, a great flurry of interest has resulted on the part of both brokers and investors. These particular options are of only one type, and it is unfortunate that a broader understanding of options in general does not exist before people rush into this phase of investing. Therefore, options in general are discussed in greater detail, and exchange-traded options are left till the end of this chapter.

If you have ever made a deposit or down payment on merchandise, say a piece of furniture that you plan to pay for in full and take delivery of at a later date, you have dealt in a form of option. Fundamentally an option is an agreement, for a fee, between a seller and a buyer to complete a transfer of property—in your case, stocks—within a specified period of time and at a specified price. The *buyer has the privilege* of either concluding the deal by fulfilling the agreement or terminating the deal by forfeiting the fee.

In the investment business, options are written for thirty, sixty, ninety, or a hundred and twenty days or six months plus ten days. As the buyer of an option, *you* determine the length of time. The longer the life of the option and the more volatile the price of the stock, the greater the chance for a change in the stock price, so you will have to pay more for a longer-term option. In any case the price of an option is only a fraction of the stock price. The exercise price is usually the same as the market price when the option is written. If you buy a six-month, ten-day call option, your profit or loss will be long-term under present tax law, while options for shorter periods are all short-term and taxed accordingly.

THE LANGUAGE OF OPTIONS

You have to know the jargon to understand how options function:

> Each option is an agreement to trade 100 shares—thus three options permit you to trade 300 shares.
>
> A *call option* is an option to buy or "call" the shares.
> A *put option* is an option to sell or "put" the shares.
> An *option writer* is the person who sells the option which may be either a call option or a put option.

As a buyer, you have the privilege of exercising the option under the terms of the agreement, but the option writer *must* abide by the agreement.

Because you can either buy or sell options, and options are *agreements* to buy (call) or sell (put) stock, you can be confused unless you understand and use the words "put" and "call" properly. First study examples of buying puts and calls as a conservative investor and as a speculator. Then consider them as a writer or seller of options.

The Option Buyer's Point of View

BUYING CALLS

Say you have studied a stock selling at 25 and concluded that, all things being equal, the stock should continue to rise. A $2,500 investment in a hundred shares over the next six months might rise to $2,800 or $2,900. But many unknown conditions might arise that would adversely affect this price move. International relations may get touchy, administrations change in Washington, the economy weaken, or other clouds appear on the horizon. Your investment may drop to $2,000.

Rather than risk a loss of $500, you decide to buy a six-month, ten-day call option for $250. If in that time the price of the stock drops, you simply do not exercise your option, and you lose only the $250 cost of the option.

On the other hand, your estimate of the stock may prove correct and the price may rise to $2,900. Before the option expires, you exercise your privilege to call the stock for $2,500. You now have $2,750 invested—the cost of the option plus the cost of the stock. At today's price, your investment shows a profit of $150. Regardless of how high the stock goes, you would only have to pay $2,750. The maximum possible loss would have been the $250 option price. In this situation, the purchase of a call option has been conservative.

In the same circumstances, the speculator would take all his investment cash—$2,750—and buy eleven call options at $250 each. Just as you stood to lose the cost of your option, so does he. The difference is that you risk only a part of your $2,750 while he risks it all. Of course, if the price goes up to 29, he will make eleven times as much as you, or a paper profit of $1,650.

If all the speculator has is $2,750, he can't very well afford to buy eleven hundred shares for $27,500 to realize his profit. The solution for him is to exercise his call option and simultaneously sell the eleven hundred shares at the market price of 29. He now owes his broker $27,500 for having exercised his call option, but his broker owes him $31,900 for the shares he sold. The speculator is due $4,400 in return for his original investment of $2,750—a gain of $1,650.

The speculator stood to gain eleven times as much as you, but he also risked losing his entire investment cash.

BUYING PUTS

Remember that a put option gives the buyer the privilege of selling stock at a specified price. Up to this point you have looked at an investment with the idea that it would increase in value. Suppose, though, you own a stock that has increased greatly in value. You now suspect it will decline over the next several months before resuming its upward climb—possibly a drop from 25 to 20. You don't care to endure the possible $500 loss; so you buy a put option for $300. This entitles you to sell a hundred shares at 25. If the price acts the way you suspect, but gives no sign of recovering, you exercise your option and sell for $2,500. This price, less the $300 option cost, is tantamount to selling for $2,200. This is better than concluding, after the price reaches 20, that you should sell.

If your original idea was correct, and the price does reach 20 and then shows signs of rebound, you can still profit by the put option. Exercising your option, you sell the stock for $2,500 and simultaneously have your broker buy one hundred shares for $2,000. This gives you a profit of $500 less the $300 option cost, and you still own the original shares, which proceed to appreciate. You have made a little more money than if you had simply watched the price go down and then go back up again.

The third possibility for the conservative investor is that the stock, instead of going down, as anticipated, may start to go up. In this case you don't exercise your put option. Granted, you forfeit the $300 option price, but for the life of the put option you have had an "insurance policy" and protection against loss.

The speculator buys a put option under the same circumstances *but* he does not already own the stock. If the price of the stock declines, he can exercise the option—as you did in the second example—by buying the stock on the market and "putting" it to the option writer. He makes a profit solely on the price of the option and has no money tied up in the stock ownership.

As with yourself, if the stock price goes up, he does not exercise his option and he loses the option price. For both of you the dollar loss was the same, but for him it was 100 per cent while yours was only 10 per cent and you still owned the stock.

Had the speculator invested as much money as you—$2,500 for your stock and $300 for the option—and bought nine options, his per cent loss would have remained the same but his dollar loss would have been much greater.

The Option Writer's Point of View

An option writer (seller) has *no choice* as to whether the option will ever be exercised. That privilege is reserved to the buyer.

WRITING CALLS

When you, an experienced investor, write a call option, you agree for a fee to sell a particular stock at a specified price. As an active but conservative investor, you study the *stock you own* and conclude that at 25 the price seems to have leveled off for the foreseeable future. You don't care to sell at this price, but if someone were to offer you 27½—$2,750—you would be glad to sell. Rather than wait for such an offer, you write a call option on your hundred shares and receive $250. If the price rises to 28 or 29, the buyer of the option is going to call the stock, and you will have to sell for $2,500. This amount, plus the $250 option price, gives you your original selling goal of $2,750.

Had the price of the stock gone down, the buyer of the call option would not call for the stock at $2,500 if he could buy it for less on the market. You, therefore, continue to own the stock and have earned an extra $250.

Writing a call option on the stock you own entails no risk of loss, but it does limit the amount of gain you can make if the price of the stock rises unexpectedly.

The speculator *does not own* the stock but regards it in the same light as you—that it is not going to go up soon. He writes a call option and, with no investment on his part, receives $250. If the stock price does not rise, the option buyer lets the option expire and the speculator keeps the price of the option.

If the stock price goes up to 29, the speculator will have to buy the stock for $2,900 in order to fulfill the terms of the option at $2,500. He loses $400 on the transaction less the $250 fee he received for the option. The more the stock price rises, the more he stands to lose.

WRITING PUTS

When you write a put option you receive a fee in return for which you are *required to buy* the stock at a specified price if the buyer so chooses. In the case of our put option, the cost of the stock is $2,500. You conclude that the stock would be a good value if you could buy it for $2,200—anything higher does not interest you. At this point you write a put option and receive $300 for it.

If the value of the stock drops to $2,000 the option holder will exercise the option, forcing you to buy for $2,500. This, less the $300, brings your cost down to $2,200. So although your stock shows a paper loss of $200, you are no further ahead or behind than if you had simply bought the stock when it reached your "good value" goal of $2,200.

On the other hand, if the stock price goes up, the option holder will not exercise it. You do not have to spend $2,500 nor do you own the stock, but you do have $300 more than you started with. The risk in writing the put option was no greater than that of buying the stock.

The speculative aspect of writing puts is the possibility of an unexpected market and stock-price drop. If it is precipitous, the option writer will have to buy the stock at a price that is now highly inflated.

CONTROLLING OPTION LOSSES

It should be noted that the speculator in options—like a professional gambler—not only takes carefully calculated risks but also provides himself with some protection against too great a loss. The technique is the stop order for the underlying stock, explained in Chapter Seven, "How to Work with Your Broker"—a *stop buy* order for call options and a *stop sell* order for put options.

The Broker's Point of View

It has been noted that options trade at only a fraction of the value of the stock represented. The broker's commission consequently is only a fraction of what it would be on a stock transaction. Whenever an option is simply allowed to expire the broker earns very little.

However, when the broker handles an option for a conservative investor he is earning a future commission if the option is exercised and the stock is actually traded. In the case of a speculator, the broker earns a *double* future commission, because the stock is bought and sold simultaneously. (The speculator must count on a big price change to afford this.) Option trading, therefore, can provide built-in commissions for the broker.

WHERE ARE THEY TRADED?

The Chicago Board of Options Exchange and the American Stock Exchange are the only formal trading locations at this time for *call* options in a limited number of stocks, and no *put* options are traded. Put options and call options not traded on these exchanges are negotiated through specialty option brokers who to all intents and purposes *provide your broker* with the functions of an exchange. You do not deal directly with these specialty brokers.

EXCHANGE TRADED OPTIONS

Call options which are traded on the C.B.O.E. and on the American Exchange vary only slightly from those traded through the specialty brokers. Most important, a continuing market is provided in which you can readily buy and sell call options prior to their expiration. Thus the investor achieves greater flexibility and is not locked into an option position.

Under present practices the expiration date of exchange-traded call options is established in January, April, July, and October. At any time you may trade an option having one of three expiration dates. As an example, in February you may select an option that expires in April or July or October. When the April expiration date passes, the July and October options will continue to be traded and a new option expiring in January of the next year will be available.

Another variation in exchange-traded call options is the exercise or "striking" price. This is usually fixed at the time trading is started in an option having a new expiration date. If the stock is selling at 25 when trading is started in an option expiring in October, then that will be the exercise price, and the option might be referred to as an Avon 25 of October. Shortly afterwards the price of Avon stock may rise to 30. Another group of Avon options will then be introduced having the same expiration dates as the first group, but the exercise price will be 30. You will then be able to trade in six different Avon options—the 25s of April, July, or October and the 30s of April, July, or October.

Stocks trading below 50 will have the exercise prices of their options set at 5-point intervals. Stocks trading between 50 and 100 will have exercise prices set at 10-point intervals; stocks trading between 100 and 200 will have 20-point intervals; and stocks trading above 200 will have option exercise prices set at 25-point intervals.

Chicago Board Options Exchange

Tuesday, February 25, 1975

Closing prices of all options. Sales unit is 100 shares. Security description includes exercise price.

	– Apr –		– Jul –		– Oct –		Stock
Option & price	Vol.	Last	Vol.	Last	Vol.	Last	Close
Aklcoa ..30	8	6¾	b	b	b	b	36¼
Alcoa .. 35	27	3⅞	22	5½	a	a	36¼
Am Tel 50	270	1½	121	2½	31	3⅛	49⅞
Am Tel 45	190	5⅛	83	5⅞	7	6⅜	49⅞
Am Tel 40	30	9½	b	b	b	b	49⅞
Atl R .. 90	260	2⅜	34	5⅝	25	7	81½
Atl R .. 80	166	7¼	33	10	a	a	81½
Avon .. 35	667	1⅞	139	3⅝	47	4½	32½
Avon .. 30	294	4⅛	93	5⅞	65	7⅛	32½
Avon 25	123	7⅝	30	9	b	b	32½
Avon 20	14	12¾	25	13½	b	b	32½
Beth S ..30	339	1½	101	2½	58	3⅜	29⅞
Beth S ..25	35	5¼	37	5¾	b	b	29⅞
Bruns .. 15	305	¼	b	b	b	b	10⅝
Bruns .. 10	260	1 7-16	160	2¼	152	2⅝	10⅝
Citicp .. 35	80	1¼	38	2⅝	25	3¾	32
Citicp .. 30	83	3⅜	18	5	2	6⅜	32
Citicp .. 25	10	7½	5	8	b	b	32
Delta .. 25	7	9¾	2	10	a	a	34⅜
Delta .. 30	60	4¾	8	6½	a	a	34⅜

17. Options Quotations

In Figure 17 you can see that there are four Avon options listed, each followed by its exercise price at 5-point intervals. The next two columns pertain to the options expiring in April and show the number of options traded during the day and the last option price. The same information is shown for options expiring in July as well as October. The last column is the closing price of the common stock covered by the option. Exchange-traded options are quoted daily along with the stock quotations in the larger papers.

Option trading should generally be left to the more sophisticated investor, but all investors should have a general idea of what options are and how they work. If you plan to try it, study it in greater depth than has been devoted to it in this chapter. The

Options Clearing Corporation has a prospectus—available from your broker—explaining exchange-traded call options in detail. Your broker can also furnish you with booklets on other call and put options. After digesting the risks and rewards, start with exchange-traded options before getting involved with put options or calls not traded on an exchange.

When you get to this point, you are strictly on your own. Happy Investing!

Random Reflections

When Macy's and Gimbel's advertise bargain prices, everyone comes to buy. When Wall Street has bargain prices, everyone leaves town. You don't have to follow the crowd.

Your portfolio is like your home. It has to suit your needs; you have to be comfortable with it; and it has to gain in value over the years.

At the end of the quarter, some mutual funds are like a push-cart vendor: busy trying to hide the dead merchandise. Look carefully before you buy.

When you get the urge to speculate, consider going to a race track instead. A few minutes after you pay your money you know the outcome—too fast to develop ulcers; no sleepless nights between start and finish; and the odds are about the same.

Don't tell me when to buy, tell me when to sell.

A doctor was quizzed at a cocktail party about many symptoms and was finally asked, "What do you suggest I do?" With no hesitation he said, "I suggest you see your doctor."

If you want reliable answers, consult your professional during working hours.

Investing is three quarters trying not to lose money and only one quarter trying to make money.

Take your profit now—capital gains taxes will be higher next year.

Investment cash is like good wine in a bottle. Neither deteriorates while you look for a good opportunity to use it.

The Three-Step-and-Stumble rule states, whenever margin requirements *or* discount rates *or* reserve requirements are raised three successive times by the monetary authorities; *look out!* Sometime—it may be a month or it may be eighteen months afterward—the market will suffer a severe setback. The reverse is not part of the rule.

Your portfolio should do better than the "averages." After all, you can always hold cash when the market drops.

About short sales: "He who sells what isn't hizn buys it back or goes to prizn."

For every investor who made a million in the market there are hundreds fighting for a comeback.

Your broker never lost money on your investments.

When you hear a "hot tip," ask the tipster how his gains compare with his losses.

Investment Clubs: Financial Communes,

Flower bonds are like fire insurance—you hope never to collect the benefits.

Until you sell, you have never had a loss or made a profit. As proof, try to declare a paper loss on your next tax return.

You wouldn't turn down a pay check because of high income taxes, so don't turn down a profit because of high capital gains taxes.

You can't take it with you and it will cost your heirs more if you try. Consult your attorney about trusts and gifts. Your heirs will love you *now.*

Mrs. Wilma Soss: management's conscience in action.

Miss Vivian Kellems: a paragon.

Top secret investment advice: buy low and sell high.

Many widows and divorcees, adequately provided for, are destitute within six to eight years.

Don't spend your principal.

"You can't have all winners!"—Tom Decker.

A to Z
Working Definitions

ACCRUED INTEREST Interest on bonds is earned daily by the bondholder and paid out every six months. The amount earned, but not paid since the last payment date, represents accrued or accumulated interest. When you buy a bond you pay the previous owner the accrued interest. On the next payment date, you receive the entire six months' interest.

ANALYSTS Individuals making detailed studies of companies or industries within the context of the current economic and political environment for the purpose of determining true investment value.

ARBITRAGE A system used by professional traders to take advantage of a disparity in the price of a stock traded on two different exchanges. Also used when there is a disparity in the prices of two securities, one of which is convertible into the other.

ASSETS Possessions of value.

CURRENT ASSETS Cash and items that may be readily converted to cash, including accounts receivable.

FIXED ASSETS Buildings, machinery etc., that are not readily convertible to cash or are required for conducting a business.

BEARER BOND See COUPON BOND.

BEAR MARKET A securities market in which prices are generally dropping. (See also BULL MARKET.)

BLOCK OF STOCK A large number of round-lot shares of stock in one company.

BLUE CHIP The stocks of a corporation having a record of superior and profitable performance over many years.

BOARD OF DIRECTORS The elected directors as a group, headed by the chairman of the board.

BOND A contractual agreement by the issuer to borrow a specified amount of money for a prescribed period of time at a given amount of annual interest. Property may be pledged to secure repayment of the borrowed money. (See also DEBENTURE and COLLATERAL.)

BOND POWER A limited power of attorney delegating legal authority to someone other than the owner to transfer the ownership of a bond.

BOOK VALUE The value of all assets—minus all liabilities and minus liquidating value of all preferred stocks—on the account books of a company. This figure is divided by the total number of shares outstanding to arrive at book value *per share*.

BROKER AS AGENT A term appearing on your confirmation of a security transaction in which your broker negotiated on your behalf with another party. (See also BROKER AS PRINCIPAL.)

BROKER AS PRINCIPAL A term appearing on your confirmation of a security transaction in which your broker bought from or sold to you from his own resources and did not negotiate the trade with another party. (See also BROKER AS AGENT.)

BULL MARKET A securities market in which prices are generally rising. (See also BEAR MARKET.)

CALLABLE A term applied to certain bonds and preferred stocks that may be redeemed at the option of the issuer under specified terms and prior to the time the issuer is legally bound to repay the money. (See also REDEMPTION PRICE and CALL PRICE.)

CALL OPTION An agreement for a fee permitting the buyer of the option to purchase stock at a specified price within a specified time. (See also PUT OPTION and Chapter Eighteen.)

CALL PRICE The price at which certain bonds and preferred stocks may be redeemed prior to mandatory redemption. (See also CALLABLE and REDEMPTION PRICE.)

CAPITAL EQUIPMENT Machinery and equipment used by a company to produce a product or provide a service.

CAPITAL GAINS The difference between the amount of capital spent to buy an investment and the amount received back when you sell. If the amount received from the sale is greater than the amount spent to purchase, it is a capital gain, otherwise it is a capital loss.

CAPITALIZATION The value of all securities issued by a corporation as shown on the financial statement. Bond value is shown as the total face value. Preferred and common stock may be shown as total par value or as "stated value." Stated value may be the actual amount received or an arbitrary amount chosen by the directors at the time the securities are issued.

CASH FLOW Net income plus depreciation. Because accounting practices permit depreciation and depletion to be computed in different ways, cash flow presumably permits fair comparisons to be made between companies.

CHURNING An *excessive* amount of trading that usually rewards the broker with greater commissions but does not bring the investor greater gains.

COLLATERAL Property pledged by a borrower to secure repayment of a loan.

COMMON STOCK A basic class of stock that is subordinate to all other classes of securities in the distribution of profits or the distribution of assets in the event of bankruptcy or liquidation of a company. A certificate represents the shares of ownership. (See also STOCKS and PREFERRED STOCK.)

CONFIRMATION A written record from a broker to the investor setting forth the details of a security transaction.

COUPON BOND A bond certificate that has coupons attached. The coupons state the amount and the date when each interest payment is due. On the due date, the coupon is cut off and sent to your bank for collection from the issuer and payment into your account. Sometimes called a bearer bond because the issuer does not record the bond owner's name nor does it appear on the bond. Whoever has possession of the bond certificate is assumed to be the rightful owner. (See also REGISTERED BOND.)

CUMULATIVE PREFERRED Stocks with a provision requiring that all preferred dividends that have been omitted be paid before any dividends are paid on common stocks.

CUMULATIVE VOTING Instead of each share of stock having one vote for each of several directors to be elected, stockholders may combine all their votes for a single director and give none to the other directors.

CURRENT RATIO A ratio of current assets to current liabilities used as a measure of the financial soundness of a company.

$$\frac{\textit{Current Assets}}{\textit{Current Liabilities}} = \textit{Current Ratio}$$ (See Chapter Thirteen.)

CYCLICAL STOCKS Stocks which over a period of several years continue to appreciate followed by several years of decline. Usually stocks of companies requiring large capital investment.

DEBENTURE A form of bond for which no collateral is pledged to secure repayment of the loan, the general credit of the company providing assurance of repayment.

DEBT FINANCING A company's method of raising cash by selling bonds, debentures, or notes. (See also EQUITY FINANCING.)

DEPLETION The dollar value of natural resources taken out of the ground owned by companies in mining, gas, or oil.

DEPRECIATION The amount by which capital equipment is reduced in value each year on the company books over the supposed useful life of the equipment. This is a bookkeeping entry and not a cash outlay. The first year 30 per cent of the value might be depreciated, the second year 20 per cent, the third year 15 per cent, etc. (See also STRAIGHT LINE DEPRECIATION.)

DIRECTORS Elected representatives of the stockholders. Directors appoint the company president, establish corporate objectives and broad corporate policy, and determine dividend policy.

DIVIDENDS A portion of a company's earnings that the Board of Directors votes to distribute pro rata, that is, to shareholders according to the shares they hold.

DOLLAR COST AVERAGING The process of investing a predetermined number of dollars at regular intervals in the stock of one company. The number of shares purchased will vary with the market price at the time of each purchase. Over a period of time the average cost will normally be lower than the market price.

EARNED SURPLUS See RETAINED EARNINGS.

EQUITY Amount of ownership represented by the common and preferred stock of a company.

EQUITY FINANCING Raising cash by selling common or preferred stock. (See also DEBT FINANCING.)

EX-DIVIDEND Synonym for "without dividend" (see Chapter Seven). On the daily stock lists, an X indicates the previous (owner) stockholder will receive the forthcoming dividend.

EXERCISE PRICE The price at which the holder of a right may purchase the security under the terms of the offering. (See Chapter Seventeen.)

FACE VALUE The dollar amount appearing on the face of a bond and indicating the amount owed by the company to the bondholder. (See also MATURITY.)

FLOAT The number of shares in a company that are in the hands of investors and available for trading.

FLOWER BONDS The name given to certain U. S. Government bonds that, in addition to being redeemable at face value upon maturity, may also be redeemed at face value to pay *federal* estate taxes upon the death of the owner even though this occurs before maturity.

GILT EDGED Bonds issued by a corporation having a superior reputation and resources to pay interest and principal as prescribed under the terms of the bond issue.

GROWTH STOCK Stock of a company whose earnings are forecast to increase at a rapid rate and usually have a history of rapid increase.

HOLDING COMPANY A corporation that owns all or at least enough stock in another corporation to control it, and does not operate any business of its own.

INDENTURE A written contract describing the complete terms of a bond issue.

INSTITUTIONAL INVESTORS Groups having huge amounts of money to invest, such as mutual funds, insurance companies, banks, retirement funds, foundations, and trusts.

INTEREST Payments a lender receives from a borrower for the use of the borrowed money.

INVESTMENT BANKER See UNDERWRITER.

LEVERAGE The process of making a small amount of cash create above-normal results. Examples of *leverage investing:* warrants, call options, buying on margin. In each case your cash outlay is much less than the value of the underlying security. As the value of the underlying investment rises or falls, the leveraged investment does also by a similar dollar amount. This dollar amount represents a larger percentage change on your small cash investment than the percentage change in value of the underlying investment.

LEVERAGED STOCK Stock of a company that has a high proportion of bonds and preferred stocks outstanding. To wit, a company with $10 million of 7 per cent bonds earns $800,000 before the $700,000 bond interest is paid; the $100,000 remains for dividends. If earnings increase 10 per cent to $880,000, then $180,000 remains for dividends after interest payments—an increase of 80 per cent. Without the bonds, an increase of 10 per cent in earnings would provide for only a 10 per cent increase in dividends.

LIABILITIES Debts owed by a company.

> CURRENT LIABILITIES All debts that become payable within one year.
>
> LONG-TERM LIABILITIES All debts, such as loans, notes, and bonds, that do not come due for full payment within one year.

LIQUIDATION The process of turning something of value into cash.

LIQUIDITY An investment condition that interests a plentiful supply of sellers and buyers; referring to a particular security issue or the market as a whole.

LISTED STOCK The stock of a company that is traded on a major security exchange and for which a registration statement has been filed with the Securities and Exchange Commission.

LONG A term denoting ownership, frequently appearing on your broker's monthly statement. (Antonym, short.)

MATURITY The date on which the money borrowed through the sale of bonds becomes due for repayment.

MONEY What we used before credit cards.

MONEY SUPPLY The amount of money in demand deposits in banks plus the cash in the hands of the public.

NET ASSET VALUE The sum of all of a company's assets less the liabilities. Mutual funds usually compute the market value of all the securities owned, subtract the liabilities, and divide this figure by the total number of shares of stock outstanding to arrive at a net asset value per share of the mutual fund.

NET CURRENT ASSETS See NET WORKING CAPITAL.

NET WORKING CAPITAL The amount of money a company has to conduct its business. This is computed by subtracting total current liabilities from total current assets. Also called NET CURRENT ASSETS or simply WORKING CAPITAL.

NET WORTH The dollar amount remaining after all liabilities have been subtracted from all assets.

NEW ISSUE Securities offered for sale to the public for the first time.

ODD LOT A quantity of shares below one hundred. Most securities are traded in units of one hundred shares. Commissions per share on smaller units are higher than on a hundred units. (See also ROUND LOT.)

ODD LOT DIFFERENTIAL The difference in price per share, when an odd lot is traded rather than a round lot. The price is usually ⅛ point higher than the round lot when purchased, and ⅛ point lower when sold.

OPTION An agreement to buy or to sell securities at a stipulated price within a specific period of time.

OPTION WRITER Individual who sells options. (See Chapter Eighteen.)

OVERBOUGHT A term applied to a particular stock or to the entire market by the investment community when it is felt that excessive buying has driven market prices above their true worth. Usually the result of overreaction by investors to *good* economic news.

OVERHEAD General continuing costs, such as taxes, supervisory salaries, and depreciation, that are incurred in the course of business regardless of productivity.

OVERSOLD See OVERBOUGHT.

PAPER PROFITS (LOSSES) A cash profit or loss does not exist until the asset has been sold. Until a sale is made, the profit or loss is simply a paper computation.

PAR VALUE The dollar amount assigned to stock by a company's charter. If there is a stock split, the par value is reduced proportionately. When the stock is initially issued, the par value, multiplied by the total shares sold, represents the accounting value of the company. As the company prospers or falters, the par value loses significance in relation to the value of the company and the market value of the stock. (See also BOOK VALUE.)

PORTFOLIO All the assets—stocks, bonds, and cash—that an individual or institution has available for investing or trading.

PRE-EMPTIVE RIGHTS A provision in company bylaws requiring a company to offer new financing to existing stockholders before an offering to the general public.

PREFERRED STOCK A class of stock having preference over common stock in the distribution of profits and in the distribution of assets in the event of bankruptcy or liquidation of a company.

PRICE/EARNINGS RATIO The P/E ratio. Current market price of a stock divided by the earnings per share for the previous twelve months.

PRIVATE PLACEMENT A security issue not offered for sale to the general public but sold to one or a small number of very large institutional investors.

PROFIT TAKING Selling securities to turn paper profits into realized cash profits.

PROSPECTUS (See Chapter Sixteen.) The first part of a corporation's registration form filed with SEC and disclosing information about the company and the securities offered for sale to the public.

PROXY Written authorization for a specified person to cast your share vote at a stockholder meeting. You may revoke a proxy at any time before the vote at the meeting and then cast your own vote, or you may specify a different person from your original choice by giving a different proxy.

PUT OPTION An agreement for a fee permitting the buyer of the option to sell stock at a specified price within a specified time. (See also CALL OPTION and Chapter Eighteen.)

QUOTATION, QUOTE The highest bid price to buy and the lowest offering price to sell a security at a given time.

REALIZED PROFITS (LOSSES)—There is no actual profit or loss until a sale has been made. The tangible profit or loss is realized when a security is sold. (See also PAPER PROFITS [LOSSES].)

REDEMPTION PRICE The price that an issuer of bonds or preferred stock must pay the owner if the security is called prior to maturity.

REFINANCING Issuing new securities and using the proceeds from their sale to pay off other securities or debts. A better interest rate or repayment terms may thus be achieved.

REGISTERED BOND A bond certificate whose owner's name is registered with the issuer and appears on the face of the certificate. The issuer pays interest when it is due by check to the registered owner. (See also COUPON BOND.)

RETAINED EARNINGS That portion of profit that a company has earned and not paid out to stockholders as dividend. Also called EARNED SURPLUS.

REVERSE SPLIT Antonym for STOCK SPLIT. Thus a one-for-five reverse split provides the shareholder with one fifth the number of shares he held but each share worth five times the value of the original shares.

ROLL OVER A loan that comes due and is immediately loaned out again under nearly the same terms. The loan is "rolled over."

ROUND LOT (A unit of one hundred shares.) Most securities are traded in this amount on the exchanges. Thus five round lots would be five hundred shares. (Occasionally if there are relatively few shares available for trading, the round lot will be fifty or ten shares.)

SEAT A colloquialism meaning membership on a security or commodity exchange.

SECONDARY OFFERING An offering of shares to the public that have previously been registered with the SEC (See Chapter Fifteen.)

SECURITIES AND EXCHANGE COMMISSION (SEC) Established by Congress to help protect investors and to curb fraudulent investment practices.

SHORT A term used to denote debt or a security to your broker. (Antonym, LONG.)

SHORT AGAINST THE BOX A form of trading used to *delay* capital gains tax. (See Chapter Seven.)

SHORT SALE Sale of borrowed stock.

SINKING FUND Money that certain bonds, debentures, or preferred stock require to be set aside for eventual redemption of the securities.

SPIN-OFF Disposal of an unwanted segment of a company's business for a price.

STOCK DIVIDEND A dividend paid in securities instead of cash. The securities may be shares of the company paying the dividend or of one of its subsidiaries.

STOCK POWER A limited power of attorney delegating legal authority to someone other than the owner to transfer ownership of stock.

STOCKS The securities comprising ownership of a corporation.

STOCK SPLIT A division of the total number of outstanding shares of stock into more shares of proportionately less value for each. A four-for-one split provides the share holder with four times the number of shares, each one quarter the value of the original share.

STRAIGHT LINE DEPRECIATION The reduction in value of the capital equipment on the books of a company by an equal amount each year over the useful life of the equipment. (See also DEPRECIATION.)

SURPLUS An accounting term for the difference between the net worth and the stated amount of capital stock.

THIN MARKET The small number of shares in a company that are in the hands of investors and available for trading. Applied to the entire market, the term means there are relatively few buyers and sellers.

THIRD MARKET Large investors in stocks of listed companies negotiate trades outside of the exchange where the stock is listed. Third market is a general term applied to the place where such trades may be negotiated.

TICKER The instrument used to report on tape the prices and the volume of security transactions to locations remote from the security exchange.

TOMBSTONE BONDS See FLOWER BONDS.

TRANSFER AGENT Usually a bank or trust company that transfers ownership of securities from the seller to the buyer by canceling an old certificate and issuing a new one. Also the agent responsible for maintaining a current list of the names and addresses of each registered shareowner of a company and the number of shares held by each.

TWO-TIER MARKET A small group of quality growth stocks consistently selling at higher price/earnings ratios than the rest of the market.

UNDERWRITER The middleman between the company issuing new securities and the investing public; also between sellers of huge blocks of stock and investors. Also known as INVESTMENT BANKER. (See also Chapter Fifteen.)

UP-TICK A trade made at a price higher than the preceding trade of the same stock. (Antonym, DOWN-TICK.)

VOLATILITY Rapid and relatively large fluctuations in the price of a security.

WORKING CAPITAL See NET WORKING CAPITAL.

WRITE-DOWN The amount by which an asset on the company books is reduced in value when it has been found to have been overstated.

WRITE-OFF The amount by which an asset is reduced in value on the company books when it has been found no longer to have any value.

XEROGRAPHY The process of making dry copies of printed material. The Haloid Corporation was a pioneer in this technology and subsequently merged to become the Xerox Corporation. Several companies now make dry copy machines, but "Xerox" copies can be made only by devices manufactured by the Xerox Corporation.

YIELD, CURRENT YIELD The income from an investment for twelve months divided by the current value of the investment expressed as per cent yield.

$$\frac{\textit{Dividends or Interest}}{\textit{Current Value}} = \textit{Per Cent Yield}$$

YIELD TO MATURITY The per cent by which your cost of a bond must change annually to reach full face value at maturity plus providing you with the annual interest income. Because bonds have different maturity dates, interest rates, and market prices, a common yardstick must be used to compare the investment value of one with another.

ZENITH Highest point or peak. The price level at which you should sell and not buy securities.

ZILLION An indefinitely large number. The amount of profit we all want from investments.

ZLOTY The monetary unit of Poland. What some of our more speculative investments are worth.

ZOOM To climb sharply. What happens to some other person's investments.

ZOUNDS A mild oath rarely used by investors when the market drops precipitously.

INDEX

Index

Index

Index

2